GROWING
BOLDER

GROWING
BOLDER

Defy the Cult of Youth, Live with Passion and Purpose

MARC MIDDLETON

To My Friend Don! Marc

RHS 2019 Nashville

GB

GROWING
BOLDER
—PUBLISHING—

Growing Bolder: Defy the Cult of Youth, Live with Passion and Purpose

Published in the United States of America by Growing Bolder Publishing with Story Farm (www.story-farm.com)

Printed in Canada.

EDITORIAL DIRECTOR Bob Morris
CREATIVE DIRECTOR Jason Farmand
CREATIVE CONSULTANT Robert Thompson
MARKETING AND PROMOTION Emily Thompson
GRAPHIC DESIGNER Ashley Heafey
COPY EDITOR Laura Paquette
PRODUCTION MANAGER Tina Dahl
INDEXING Amy Hall

Library of Congress Cataloging-in-Publication data available upon request.

ISBN: 978-0-9849300-1-2

First edition: January 2019

10 9 8 7 6 5 4 3 2 1

PUBLISHER'S NOTE The purpose of this book is to educate and entertain. Neither the author nor the publisher is engaged in rendering health, legal, financial, psychological, nutritional or medical advice and this book is not intended as a substitute for the advice of a competent professional. The reader should consult an appropriate professional before starting any program to determine if it is right for your individual needs. The author and publisher make no representations or warranties with respect to the accuracy or completeness of the contents of this work and specifically disclaim any liability to any party for any loss, damage or disruption that is a consequence of the use and application of the contents of this book or is caused by errors or omissions, whether such errors or omissions result from accident, negligence, or any other cause.

For KELSEY *and* QUINN.

You've given me countless
moments of joy.

I'd love to give you a better culture
to grow old in.

Or at least a better way to grow old
in the culture we have.

66 I have worked with everyone from Martha Stewart to Dr. Oz, who are no strangers to the anti-aging movement, but Marc Middleton is the rock star. I'm buying this book for everyone I know."

—**Lisa Lynn**, *best-selling author ("The Metabolism Solution"), fitness expert and founder of LynFit Nutrition*

66 Read with caution. 'Growing Bolder' is a wrecking ball of truth and inspiration that just might smash everything you think you know about getting older. Marc's mission to 'Rebrand Aging' represents a desperately needed paradigm shift that should be shouted from the rooftops of society and shared with the young and old alike."

—**Cody Sipe Ph.D.**, *professor, fitness pioneer, co-founder of the Functional Aging Institute*

66 Having had the privilege of working with thousands of cancer survivors over many years I know firsthand the power of passion and purpose. Marc has personally impacted my life in profound ways and I am so excited for all those who will benefit from the lessons of this book."

—**Doug Ulman**, *president and CEO of Pelotonia, former president and CEO of Livestrong*

CONTENTS

CONTENTS

CONTENTS

CHAPTER 1

THE BACKSTORY

―

> Do not let your fire go out, spark by irreplaceable spark in the hopeless swamps of the not-quite, the not-yet, and the not-at-all. Do not let the hero in your soul perish in lonely frustration for the life you deserved and have never been able to reach. Check your road and the nature of your battle. The world you desired can be won, it exists, it is real, it is possible, it's yours.
>
> —AYN RAND

OVER THE YEARS, PEOPLE HAVE OFTEN ASKED, "When are you going to write the book on Growing Bolder?" I knew I'd write it someday, but I've long been bothered by people who brand themselves experts before they actually know much about the topics upon which they expound. The world is filled with self-proclaimed subject-matter experts who are eager to tell us how to accomplish things that they've never accomplished themselves.

Even after I had devoted more than a decade developing the concept of Growing Bolder — and could clearly see the benefits of adopting a Growing Bolder lifestyle for people of all ages — I didn't want to write a book until I felt I had something valuable to add to the conversation. I didn't want to simply repeat what others had said in a different context, or to aggregate the results of multiple studies that reinforced my personal beliefs. I wanted to bring something new to the party.

And I wanted to write it myself. I've been approached by several publishers, and when I told them that I wasn't ready to write a book, they responded incredulously: "You don't need to actually write it. We'll take care of that part." Such a suggestion always made me laugh, because no one else could have written this book.

Malcolm Gladwell's book *Outliers* suggests that 10,000 hours spent learning a subject is required before one can call oneself an expert. I've averaged 60 hours a week for the past 12 years on the Growing Bolder project. That's more than 37,000 hours of researching, interviewing, reading, writing, thinking and doing — actually applying what I've learned to my own life.

Almost every person mentioned in this book has been featured on the Growing Bolder media platform. We have conducted thousands of interviews with doctors, scientists, researchers, global thought leaders, celebrities and ordinary people living extraordinary lives, all with a sharp focus on understanding and sharing the secrets to growing older with passion and purpose.

When I became confident that I had something valuable to say, I was determined to say it in a way that didn't read like an academic research paper, as many books about aging and longevity do. As important as some of these books may be, most readers aren't interested in detailed research studies. They want to know the ways in which they're personally impacted by the negativity that underpins the culture of aging in the U.S. More importantly, they want to know what they can do about it. They want a pathway to results.

This book is that pathway, whether you're a 35-year-old realizing for the first time that you're getting older; a 55-year-old wondering what's next; a 65-year-old wondering if there even is a what's next; or a 75– or 85-year-old searching for purpose and meaning in a new life stage filled with nearly limitless possibilities.

Growing Bolder reveals how the "Machine," a powerful combination of corporate, media, private and governmental forces, wants you to feel worn, weak and worthless and is spending billions every month to back campaigns of disinformation and despair. You'll learn how we are all victims of a form of cultural brainwashing that is stealing years from our lives and quality of life from our years. You'll learn how some leaders of the anti-ageism movement are actually promoting an ageist message. You'll learn why retirement is an outdated concept, why risk-taking is essential as we age and how to imagine and then create what's next in your own life. You'll discover the power of prehabilitation and how to leverage the health-wealth connection to dramatically reduce your future health-care costs. You'll learn the secrets of active longevity from the "Rock Stars of Aging," and how to orchestrate a "good death." Finally, this book will share the art of the Growing Bolder come-back — a playbook for making the rest of your life the best of your life.

Changing the culture of aging in an extremely ageist society is a monumental challenge that many believe isn't possible to accomplish. Most leaders of the anti-ageism movement say we can't do it alone. They say we need policy change and institu-tional change. They say we must bring government and private enterprise along with us. They say we must engage younger people in our struggle.

I disagree. I believe we must change as individuals. We must work toward the goal of cultural transformation one life at a time. Waiting for policy change and culture change is simply another cop out — an excuse to sit back and wait for the world we desire to come to us. And the truth is, it won't get here soon enough to help any of us.

That doesn't mean we shouldn't try to change the way the world views people over a certain age, institutions treat them or corporations value them. It doesn't mean that we shouldn't support organizations that are working to facilitate cultural change. It simply means we can't change societal belief systems until we change our own, because our minds play host to a virulent, ageist pathogen that grows more powerful as we grow older. Our personal belief system is either the path-way through which this pathogen enters or our defense system against it.

If we can change our belief system about aging, we can change the trajectory of our lives. If enough of us can make that change, large-scale cultural change will follow. It's my sincere hope that this book will be the beginning of such a change for you.

CHAPTER 2

THE GROWING BOLDER GENESIS

——

*Taking a Leap of Faith and
Becoming a Man on a Mission*

66
——
*Come to the edge, Life said.
They said: We are afraid.
Come to the edge, Life said.
They came. It pushed them . . .
And they flew."*
—GUILLAUME APOLLINAIRE

LIKE EVERYONE WHO DOESN'T WANT TO BELIEVE that life after 60 or 70 is a slippery slope into the grave, I've often wondered: "What's next?" After decades of working in broadcast news, I had no plans to retire — but I didn't want to work for "the man" the rest of my life. I wanted my "what's next" to be something that I was passionate about, something that provided the kind of autonomy that working for someone else doesn't offer, something that made a difference in the lives of others.

I wondered what I might do or create that would leverage my skills and allow me to control my destiny into my 60s, 70s, 80s and beyond. It's obvious to anyone who's even remotely paying attention that we have ageist workplaces nestled within an ageist culture that is supported and reinforced by an enthusiastically ageist media. None of this is good news in a country with a rapidly aging population. And it certainly wasn't good news in my industry. I had been a sports and news anchor for nearly 3 decades. I was an aging bald man with a big salary in an industry that loves fresh faces anxious to work for small paychecks. In other words, I had a big target on my back.

As I pondered future possibilities, my industry was undergoing rapid transformations. With the number of content channels exploding exponentially, viewership on any one channel declined, and advertisers began diverting budgets to digital platforms. With revenue declining and viewing patterns changing, the definition of news itself began to change.

Enterprise reporting, investigative reporting and feature storytelling were regarded as luxuries that very few stations could or would support. "Breaking news" quickly became the lifeblood of local TV as stations began reporting almost exclusively on murders, mobile-home fires, armed robberies, home invasions and drug deals gone bad. In a very short time, local news became, for the most part, a never-ending crime report. Communities across the U.S. began to feel like dark, dangerous and dirty places.

When I no longer allowed my children to watch their dad on TV, I came to realize — with great pain — that I no longer wanted local news to be the profession that defined me or consumed my creative energies. My desire to identify "what's next" became a focused mission over the next two years.

The Market Research Question that Started it All

About the same time, station management shared its latest audience research with me. I couldn't get past one of the very first questions on the viewer survey: "How old are you?" In reality, it wasn't the question that concerned me. It was the fact that the station immediately discontinued the interview when the answer was any age over 55.

I knew from previous research that the average age of our viewers was 57, so I asked management why we didn't care about the opinions of our average viewers. "It's not that we don't care," I was told. "Advertisers don't care. We need to attract and retain the audience they want. We need to focus all our energy on attracting viewers 25 to 54. That's where the game is played."

That conversation provided the spark that started it all. I became obsessed with this shortsighted demographic disconnect: a major miscalculation by several very large and influential industries. Why would we *not* care about the opinions of our largest audience constituency? The size of this demographic group was undeniable. So, I assumed that there must be something about the way people aged 55 or older spend —

or don't spend — that fails to interest advertisers.

I dedicated the better part of the next year studying the 76 million baby boomers born between 1946 and 1964, a generation that has transformed every life stage as its aged, a generation that demographers have described as a pig going through a python.

I realized that I was supposed to dread aging but I didn't. And I knew that I wasn't alone. To borrow a phrase from Dylan Thomas, it was clear that many baby boomers weren't going gentle into that dark night. I became convinced, with complete certainty, that boomers would instead use inevitable advances in medicine and technology to not only transform a life stage but to create a new life stage that would change the face of aging forever.

I learned that consumers aged 50-plus — the same group advertisers and media organizations were ignoring — in fact had more money than any "senior" population in history, controlling more than 70 percent of the nation's discretionary income and accounting for nearly $4 trillion in wealth. And, in an unprecedented transfer of wealth, they were in line to inherit another $15 trillion over the next 20 years.

Not only did older people have money, they were spending it — dominating 119 out of the top 123 consumer packaged goods (CPG) categories. Yet, despite the age group's size, wealth and spending habits, fewer than 5 percent of all advertising dollars were directed toward this demographic. And those dollars were disproportionately spent on pharmaceutical and insurance ads. Obviously, the assumption was that the future of people 50 and older would consist of little more than getting sick and dying. But it wasn't only advertisers who held this view. The broader culture seemed to agree.

I wasn't buying any of it. I believed we would spend at unprecedented levels in unprecedented ways in the years and decades ahead: on travel, technology, entrepreneurial ventures, smart homes and — most significantly — life-enhancing experiences. I believed that for many, this new life stage would embody the spirit of the late Hunter S. Thompson, who wrote: "Life should not be a journey to the grave with the intention of arriving safely in a pretty and well preserved body, but rather to skid in broadside in a cloud of smoke, thoroughly used up, totally worn out, and loudly proclaiming 'Wow! What a ride!'"

Making the most of that ride would require a certain degree of health and wellbeing, adequate finances, a strong social circle, a passion for adventure and a willingness to engage in the kind of personal risk-taking thought to be appropriate only for younger people. Mostly, it would require a new belief system.

While still at the TV station, I did what I still do to this day — use my position in the media to interview those from whom I hope to learn. Abigail Trafford, an award-winning journalist at The Washington Post, had just written "My Time: Making the Most of the Bonus Decades After 50." I was, at the time, trying to persuade the station to let me produce a series of stories about the changing culture of aging. I figured that an interview with Trafford would aid those efforts.

When I asked her on camera about the impact of the impending age wave, her answer was powerful and profound. "I'm a journalist," she said. "I know what a big story is. The creation of an entirely new life stage is not just a big story; it is the biggest story of our time. We'll look back in 200 years and understand that it had the most significant and lasting impact on our species of any other event during our lives."

It was a great sound bite. But it did nothing to change the mind of management, who were convinced that creating an on-air franchise targeting those not in the "prime demo" would drive away viewers and advertisers.

I scheduled a meeting with the 60-year-old publisher of our local newspaper, one of several big city dailies owned by Tribune Publishing. Certainly, I thought, she'd understand the value of older consumers and be interested in a regular column about growing older with passion and purpose. After all, she was part of the generation that grew up with newspapers and still liked holding newsprint in their hands.

I couldn't have been more wrong. She didn't even feign interest. "How can you not care about the majority of your readers?" I asked. She answered with dismissive authority: "Our older readers aren't going anywhere. We won't lose them, so we don't need to cater to them. However, we need to do everything possible to retain and attract younger readers — and any content that targets older readers is a huge turnoff."

I was dumbfounded. Realizing that I'd never have an opportunity to provide content to the paper — at least not under this publisher — I didn't hesitate to disagree. "Taking older consumers for granted is the worst business decision that any leader can make, especially one in the media business," I replied. "They'll grow increasingly comfortable with getting their news online and begin cancelling subscriptions as quickly as the younger readers you're so desperate to retain." With subscriptions and advertising rates declining, the publisher retired within a year, noting that "the business has changed."

It was certainly a contrarian business perspective, but I became convinced that celebrating the opportunities of aging and building the world's first active-lifestyle brand targeting the 50-plus market was a worthy mission. I was definitely focused on baby boomers, but my interest wasn't in a single demographic group that would one day be gone. I was drawn to the opportunity of a new life stage that had the potential to improve the lives of everyone, forever.

I clearly saw the very real possibility of living lives of passion and purpose into our 80s, 90s and 100s. It was a very different vision than the one I had been exposed to from the moment I could look at picture books or observe my aging grandparents. I didn't accept the inevitability of disability and morbidity that was universally portrayed on television. Nor did I accept the inevitability of sadness, loneliness and even ugliness that advertising campaigns had warned me of for decades.

I saw age not as a disease, but as an opportunity. That vision, combined with the emerging digital revolution, provided the pathway to create a business and build a brand. Suddenly, the media gatekeepers were gone. Broadcasting was becoming narrowcasting, and the need for content was greater than ever. It was now possible for anyone to start his or her own online media network. "That would be a very bold move," I thought to myself. "Especially at my age." That's the moment that the name Growing Bolder came to me and told me what I had to do. It cut through the fear and connected with the badassery that lives inside us all. It's the key to overcoming ageism and living with passion and purpose at any age.

The name crystalized the concept and without hesitation I made what can only be described as a Growing Bolder move. I walked into the president and general manager's office and resigned from what had been the best job of my life.

I left behind a 25-year career that some might describe as glamorous and well paid. I took a leap of faith without a parachute, but with belief in my dream, a strong work ethic and an undeniable feeling that the universe would catch me on the way down.

For the first time in decades, I was no longer a TV news or sports anchor. I was an unemployed 58-year-old determined to stop simply growing older and start Growing Bolder. I was a man on a mission to change the aging narrative from limitation to liberation, from challenge to opportunity, from weakness to power, from fear and regret to passion and purpose. I was determined to disconnect from the ageist propaganda machine so pervasive in our culture and begin deprogramming the world from the insidious cult of youth.

How's that for a "what's next"?

CHAPTER 3

A TALE OF TWO FUTURES

The Best of Times and the Worst of Times

> **"** *Whether it's the best of times or the worst of times, it's the only time we've got.*
> —ART BUCHWALD

IN THE OPENING PARAGRAPH OF *A Tale of Two Cities*, Charles Dickens wrote: "It was the best of times, it was the worst of times ... it was the spring of hope, it was the winter of despair, we had everything before us, we had nothing before us."

Aging is very much a tale of two cities. The 50-plus demographic is the most diverse group of all time, containing extreme wealth and abject poverty, vibrant health and chronic illness and disability.

On one hand, this is the greatest time in the history of humankind to be over 50, 80, and even 100. We've all won the Mega-Life Lottery. Humankind has been on the planet for 300,000 years and, for 99 percent of that time, the average life expectancy was 18. In 1900, the average life expectancy in the U.S. was just 49, and there were only 122,000 people 85 or older. It's projected that there'll be nearly 20 million 85 or older by 2050. Source: U.S. Census Bureau

Of the 117 billion people born since the beginning of time, fewer than 3 billion have lived with a life expectancy greater than 50 and a daily income greater than $2.50. We're all in that group! Very few in the history of humankind have ever made it to our age with an opportunity for continued adventure and significance.

Ray Kurzweil, Google's director of engineering and one of the world's foremost futurists, says we've lost perspective when it comes to appreciating what we have. "Read about what human life was like two centuries ago," he told me. "Read Thomas Hobbes. Read Charles Dickens. Life expectancy was 37. Franz Schubert died at 31. Mozart died at 35. There were widespread bacterial infections. There were no antibiotics. Life was extremely harsh, filled with hard labor. It took six to eight hours just to prepare the evening meal. The poor today have amenities that kings and queens didn't have a century ago. We very quickly forget what life was like not long ago."

Thanks to advances in medicine, healthcare, technology and genetic research—as well as improved personal lifestyle choices — there now exists an entirely new life stage. We have a two-, three- or even four-decade opportunity for meaningful, fulfilling life beyond what had been considered normal retirement age. This new life stage offers nearly limitless opportunities to reinvent yourself, pursue your passions, return to school, start a business, repair old relationships, build new relationships, give back to your community and leave a meaningful legacy.

We're no longer constrained to living linear lives, in which our activities must reflect our ages. We can go to college at 50, get married at 60, start a business at 70, begin running at 80, take up acting at 90 and write a book at 100. There are no longer any arbitrary, age-related rules as to what's possible and acceptable at any stage of our lives. These extra decades can be filled with passion, purpose and possibility.

The odds of living to an active 100 are increasing every day. Of course, hitting the century mark is worthwhile only if we can get there in a physical, mental and emotional state that allows us to enjoy it. Without quality of life, longevity is more punishment than opportunity. No one wants to become a centenarian if all it means is living an additional 20 years in lonely isolation: bedridden, drugged and being attended to by strangers who might care *for* you but don't really care *about* you.

But what if we can remain active into our 100s? What if we can continue growing, laughing, learning, loving, sharing and giving back into our 100s? What if the growing number of scientists and researchers who predict that living to 120 *and enjoying it* will soon be commonplace are right? What if tomorrow's 100-year-olds aren't warehoused like many 80-year-olds are today? What if they're not a financial drain on their families and society as a whole? What if they need far less healthcare than the average 40-year-old now requires? What if they're working, dancing, swimming, volunteering, living alone and enjoying amazing meals and fabulous vacations? Longevity can be a great thing.

The Worst of Times

The best-of-times scenario is the beginning of an unprecedented period of active longevity. In the worst-of-times scenario, we're at the beginning of an unimaginable nightmare of elder warehouses: a rapidly aging society of poor, sick people with no savings and no long-term care insurance trying to survive in an ageist world in which healthcare costs are dramatically escalating.

While there's no debate that we're on the cusp of a longevity revolution, life expectancy for Americans has recently dropped for the first time in decades.

According to the World Health Organization, there are now more than 30 countries where life expectancy is higher than it is in the U.S. This is a shameful statistic for the wealthiest nation on earth. The decline is directly related to a rise in preventable chronic disease, drug overdoses and suicides.

The U.S. suicide rate for older people, essentially stable for six decades, has surged in the past 15 years, according to a study by the National Center for Health Statistics. The rise in these deaths of despair is especially steep among adults age 45 to 64, where suicide rates are up 63 percent for women and 43 percent for men.

The highest suicide rate in the U.S. is for white men over 85. This is due to many factors, including low socialization and lack of physical activity. Some say it's because the elderly usually don't fail when they attempt suicide. They use guns more often than younger people, and advanced age lowers the likelihood of surviving serious injury. The more important question to ask is this: Why are these people putting guns to their heads in the first place?

White men over 85 grew up in a sexist, racist and ageist society — but were never part of any group that was discriminated against. They haven't developed the coping skills and resilience that most women and minorities have needed to navigate their daily lives. For the first time, they're considered to be "less than." They're now the victims of institutionalized ageism. They're now feeling the devastation of being devalued.

We can expect to see a continuous increase in the already alarming suicide rates of people middle-aged and older. That's because we're all victims of the greatest brainwashing job in the history of mental manipulation. An ageist propaganda machine has programmed us to literally destroy ourselves from the inside out as we age.

We live in an increasingly age-segregated society. Our culture is fine with putting us into understaffed nursing facilities where we're alive but not engaged in life in any meaningful way. It's preparing us to accept this fate by convincing us that we're destined to become weak and sickly, and will soon have little of importance to contribute. It's conditioning us to believe that we're becoming burdens whose value to society has passed. It's telling us that we've lived our lives, had our chances and it's time now to begin to withdraw. It's telling us that if we can't afford anything better, there are warehouses in which we can await death.

Growing old in an ageist culture is like being profiled by the police, stopped without reason and charged for crimes that we didn't commit. We're automatically guilty of every negative stereotype associated with aging simply because of birth dates. Why is this acceptable when age doesn't predict performance or represent value more accurately than gender or race?

Some of us just aren't interested in knowing the truth about what's possible as we age. We want to believe that we're beyond the age of possibility, and that our productive time has drawn to a close. We're tired of trying and failing. New opportunities represent only new opportunities for disappointment. We take comfort in believing that it's too late to reinvent ourselves, to pursue missed opportunities and to cultivate new passions. We're trapped in what amounts to a slow death spiral and, tragically, many of us are OK with that. Like an elderly inmate who doesn't want to be paroled, we've come to find comfort in the cages that confine us. Those cages are our belief systems about aging.

To change the way we age, we must change the way we think about aging. Perceptions drive outcomes. Growing Bolder is about removing the shackles of a damaging belief system and escaping the cage. It's about disconnecting from the ageist propaganda machine, overcoming its debilitating brainwashing and reprogramming ourselves to embrace the nearly limitless opportunities of growing older.

A new belief system about what's possible as we age is the foundation upon which this entire book is built. It's the key to Growing Bolder and the pathway to active longevity. But a new belief system, no matter how powerful, isn't enough. We must act upon that new belief system. A change in belief without a change in behavior simply won't get it done. Both are required.

More than anything else, it's fear that puts us on the couch and all but ensures a life of dwindling significance and enjoyment. Action is the antidote to fear. Action is at the core of the Growing Bolder ethos.

We won't live the engaged, social, passionate, rewarding, exciting, adventurous lives that we were meant to live if we can't overcome fear. We must take action. Living a big bold life into our 90s and 100s isn't an outlandish, unachievable dream. It's an opportunity. We must want it, and then go get it. Calculated, strategic risk-taking has always been, and always will be, the path to success.

We can't wait for our culture to change. We can't wait for the healthcare system to change. We can't wait for employers to change. We must change our belief systems and then fearlessly take control of our lives through action and persistence. We must start Growing Bolder.

CHAPTER 4

WE'VE ALL BEEN BRAINWASHED

—

Disconnecting From the Life-Limiting Message of the "Machine"

> 66
> —
> *Of all the self-fulfilling prophecies in our culture, the assumption that aging means decline and poor health is probably the deadliest.*
> —MARILYN FERGUSON

WHEN I BEGAN THINKING ABOUT BUILDING a business around Growing Bolder, I registered trademarks, purchased web domains and learned how to use software programs such as Photoshop and Dreamweaver so I could create graphics and build a website.

I was convinced there was a significant opportunity to create a valuable brand with the potential to inspire millions and help transform what the world thought about growing older. I was totally energized by the idea. Yet, it took me nearly six years to walk away from my job and get started.

I hesitated not for a lack of belief in the idea but for a lack of belief in myself— more specifically, a lack of belief in my *future* self. The more seriously I thought about making a change, the louder the voice inside my head screamed: "You won't have the time, the money, the stamina or the skills to see this through. This is a foolish idea. You'll lose your life savings and destroy your family."

Why was I suddenly afraid when, for decades, I had taken pride in being fearless? Why did I fear failure when I could so clearly imagine success? Why was I feeling over the hill, when I had never considered that there *was* a hill? Why was I timid, when self-confidence had never been a problem? And why were all the objections being offered by the voice inside my head age-related? What was *that* about?

Was I *really* too old to reinvent myself as a successful, first-time entrepreneur? Was my vision bigger than my ability? Was I already over the hill and tiptoeing toward decline?

That's when I understood that I had been brainwashed. I was the unwitting victim of a systematic, decades-long propaganda campaign designed to make me afraid. I was being influenced by a particularly devious form of deception.

In that moment, it was clear to me that the reason I needed to quit my job and start this new business was the very reason I thought that I *couldn't* quit my job and start this new business. I was about to be trapped inside a cage of my own construction; an internalized belief system was controlling my thoughts and undermining my future. I was being controlled by the "Machine" — the cultural consciousness we live within.

Boom! There it was — the intersection of need and opportunity. Growing Bolder was even more important than I had realized. It was far more than just a good idea for what might become a great business. It was the key to unlocking my cage and escaping a fear mongering, ageist propaganda machine and the toxic belief system it so effectively promotes.

The Machine has many voices: politicians, advertisers, economists, healthcare providers, media companies, social planners and the guy next door. The Machine's message, in a nutshell, is that aging is an incurable social ill, a drain on society, an insult to true beauty and something to be feared and ashamed of.

We Value Life By The Way We Live It

The average human lives about 28,000 days. And days, like any commodity, become more valuable as their quantity decreases. When it comes to time, however, the Machine wants us to believe just the opposite. It begins devaluing each successive day beyond what it considers our "prime." This may be the most damaging, life-limiting lie inflicted upon us. We're not meant to live lives of decreasing value. We're here to live momentous lives — to seize each moment and to value every breath.

When we know with certainty that we have more yesterdays

than tomorrows, something important happens, or it should. We need to hear the clock ticking but not be overwhelmed by the sound. Why is it that so many need a cancer diagnosis or a near-death experience to understand the value of every moment? The older we get, the more aware we become of the time we've wasted. For most, that is a disheartening realization. For some, it becomes a powerful and potentially life-transforming motivation.

We value life by the way that we live it, by the choices that we make. I knew that if I couldn't find the courage to start Growing Bolder in my own life, that I'd never be able to persuade anyone else to. Before this moment of clarity was gone, I forced myself to the edge and jumped. I quit my job and started to remedy my flawed, life-limiting belief system about aging.

Our Future Negative Self-Image

Dr. Maxwell Maltz, who wrote the 1960 best-seller *Psycho-Cybernetics*, talked about the power and the importance of self-image. Dr. Maltz defined the mind-body connection as the key to success in attaining personal goals. His work became the foundation upon which Zig Ziglar, Brian Tracy, Tony Robbins and many other self-help and motivational gurus have based their teachings.

Dr. Maltz suggested ways to bolster individual self-image. And his work all but created the field of sports psychology by identifying the power of visualization — a technique now employed by nearly every world-class athlete.

But what Dr. Maltz didn't say — and what few have said since — is that in addition to our current self-image, we have a future, age-related self-image taking shape in our subconscious. Our two self-images exist simultaneously and can be wildly divergent; a current self-image of power and success belies a future self-image of fear and weakness.

The poisonous seed of this future self-image is planted when we're infants, and watered and fertilized throughout our lives by that relentless propaganda machine. It begins to assert itself when we first feel the effects of age and the sting of ageism, often in our 30s or 40s. From that moment on, our current self-image — however strong it may be — begins to slowly erode and is eventually replaced.

Ageism is defined as the stereotyping, prejudice and discrimination against people on the basis of their age. It can involve discrimination against young people, but it typically refers to the treatment of older people because of its insidious nature and harmful effects on their health. Unlike racism and sexism, ageism is unique in targeting our future selves, which is why older people are often deeply ageist, having internalized a lifetime of negative stereotypes about aging.

By the time children are 3 years old, most already have an extremely negative image of aging. Not surprising, since multiple studies examining the portrayal of age in hundreds of picture books reveal that nearly all children's books published in the '60s, '70s and '80s promoted ageist attitudes and contained demeaning stereotypes of older people. (Ansello, 1977; Ansello, 1988; James & Kormanski, 1999; McGuire, 2005).

Older characters either didn't exist or were totally inconsequential to the plot. If they appeared at all, they were depicted as "dull, inarticulate, unoriginal, noncreative and boring." There was no indication that aging was a natural and lifelong process. There were no examples of capable older workers or older community leaders.

Separate studies in 1976 and 1984 revealed that young children internalize these demeaning and ageist messages at a very young age and have difficulty even thinking about growing old themselves, describing older adults as "shorter, dirtier, uglier, less healthy and less helpful" than younger adults. This not only makes the young disrespect the old, it also instills a deep-seated fear of aging. The Machine preys upon that fear for a lifetime.

Television is the most pernicious instrument of our ageist cultural brainwashing. From the moment TV programs began appearing in our living rooms in the early- to mid 1950s, older people have been underrepresented and misrepresented — portrayed almost exclusively as frail, feeble and forgetful. What makes this ageist messaging more credible — and therefore more destructive — is that it is often skillfully woven into content that may otherwise be entertaining, educational and even inspirational. The poison pill has been coated with sugar.

These days, TV success has little to do with the quality of the program, or even the number of viewers. Programs are often cancelled not because audiences are too small, but because they're too old — and therefore deemed unworthy by marketers. If you can't attract the coveted 25- to 54-year-old viewer, odds are that you won't find a home on network television.

Worse than the programs themselves are the multimillion-dollar advertising campaigns designed to make us dread aging by offering "anti-aging" and "age defying" products while suggesting that "60 is the new 30" or "70 is the new 40" — as if there is something inherently wrong with being 60 or 70.

The bottom line: We are being hypnotized so we can be monetized. Ageism has become a profitable business model. Social scientists tell us that cultural hypnosis takes place over a long period of time, with suggestions coming not from a single voice or a single source but from nearly every form of media. Cultural hypnosis, unlike individual hypnosis for therapy or entertainment, doesn't require a willing participant.

This phenomenon is fueled by constant bombardment from the sophisticated 30-second "hypnosis sessions" known as commercials:

Close your eyes and listen to the sound of our narration. Look at the images in our ad. Read the words on our page. Observe the people in our video. You are getting old and weak and ugly. You are tired and unhappy. Getting old is a disgrace. Only our product, our medicine or our service can make you strong, attractive and desirable. When this commercial is over, you will be compelled to feel inadequate and unhappy. You will believe that our product is your salvation. You will give us your money.

The anti-aging youth movement created by advertisers plays upon our fears and insecurities, cultivating dissatisfaction and self-hate. They want us to believe that wrinkles, gray hair and age spots depreciate us like a beat-up old car that's no longer reliable — an embarrassment to the entire neighborhood when parked in the driveway. Self-acceptance is their enemy, and the ruination of their business. That's why they'll stop at nothing to make us dissatisfied with ourselves.

According to Forbes, the median age of creative staffers in advertising agencies is 25. Just 5 percent of agency employees are over 50, and few of them work in creative capacities. Of course, the thinking goes, you don't *need* to be older to understand older people — just like you don't need to have been a football player to be a football coach. But it sure helps.

Given the age of those who develop creative campaigns, it isn't surprising that older people remain dramatically underrepresented and misrepresented by TV programs. When they do appear, they're typically portrayed as buoyantly happy (because they use a certain product) or as ridiculous and insulting stereotypes. The running cast of older characters includes: Mr. Memory Loss, Mrs. Crepey Skin, Mr. I Hate My Gray Hair, Mrs. I've Fallen and I Can't Get Up and Mr. I Can't Get It Up But Sure Wish I Could.

Corporate greed, combined with the sophistication of targeted marketing, has played a large part in creating distinct micro-generations that are valued primarily because of their spending habits. Age has become a force that separates us.

We older people are not without blame. While we didn't create the ageist propaganda machine, we became one of its greatest promoters during our adolescence. The counterculture we created in the '60s has come back to haunt us. We're now reaping what we sowed decades ago, when we proclaimed we'd never trust anyone over 30 and only the good die young.

When Paul McCartney wrote, "Will you still need me, will you still feed me, when I'm 64?" we imagined 64 as an age of decrepitude and dependence. We romanticized the virtues of youth while repudiating the value of age. We created the generational divide — and cast a disdainful and unappreciative eye on the other side. Everything looks very different now that we've *reached* the other side. Our Summer of Love has become our Winter of Despair.

Books and TV aren't the only purveyors of age-related discontent. Radio, magazines, billboards, newsletters, emails, social media, chats with friends and co-workers and overheard conversations are complicit. It's comedians telling ageist jokes, over-the-hill greeting cards, coffin-shaped gift boxes for 50th birthdays, mandatory retirement ages and doctors prescribing medication before lifestyle modification. It's a never-ending chorus that's impossible to ignore, and whose influence is difficult to overstate.

Dr. Robert Butler, president of the International Longevity Center and the person who coined the term "ageism" 35 years ago, told "Growing Bolder Radio" shortly before his death in 2010, "We are witness to, and even unwitting daily participants in, cruel imagery, jokes, language and attitudes directed at older people."

Our disdain for the elderly is reflected in every industry and institution. One disheartening example is the fact that only about 10 percent of U.S. medical schools require training in geriatric medicine. As a result, only 1 percent of medical students choose geriatric medicine as a specialty. The American Geriatrics Society says there are only about 7,600 certified geriatric specialists nationwide — one for every 2,000 Americans over the age of 75 and estimates that at least 36,000 geriatric specialists will be needed by 2030.

Of course, you can't force medical students to practice specialties that don't interest them. But failure to expose medical students to the fastest-growing need and opportunity in medicine — and allowing them to view the elderly exclusively through the prism of our youth-obsessed culture — is unquestionably ageist.

Ageism has infiltrated every part of our society and every corner of our consciousness. And its message of disease and despair has been internalized. Multiple research studies have proven that subconscious "age stereotypes," formed in our youth and reinforced daily for decades, determine to a large extent how we age and how long we live.

We've come to accept the contention that age is a disease —

and we're its victims. We've been programmed to believe that when our skin begins to wrinkle, our dreams begin to die. It's a diagnosis that's self-confirmed with every gray hair and every ache and pain, and every time we lose or forget something.

The moment we accept an idea as fact, the words and images that surround and support that notion become real — and have the same power over us as truth. The negative stereotypes of aging are so deeply embedded in our national psyche that we've come to fear what can, in reality, be the best years of our lives.

Close your eyes and visualize someone in their 90s. What do you see? Someone actively engaged in life: working, traveling, socializing, writing, painting, dancing and volunteering? Or someone strapped to a bed in a nursing home with little to no quality of life. We see examples of both every day.

If, when you close your eyes and imagine someone who is 90, you see someone isolated, bedridden, addled and barely able to move, then you should be very concerned about your own future. Because the most important lifestyle determinant that dictates how we age is neither diet nor exercise; it's our basic belief system about aging. What the mind believes, the body embraces — and we're the unwitting victims of an ageist propaganda campaign that penetrates and permeates every part of our society.

We are, in fact, aged less by our years and more by our beliefs. Dr. Deepak Chopra, a pioneer in integrative medicine, personal transformation and mind-body healing told me: "We age because we believe we are supposed to age. The mass consciousness of aging has been bought into, and because we believe the illusion, we age accordingly. We have the potential to add up to 30 years to our lives by simply modifying our belief systems about aging." Similarly, a 2002 study, conducted by Dr. Becca Levy at the Yale University School of Public Health and published in the Journal of Personality and Social Psychology, found that "Individuals with more positive self-perceptions of aging, measured up to 23 years earlier, lived 7.5 years longer than those with less positive perceptions."

A positive perception about aging not only leads to a longer life, it helps us bounce back more quickly and more fully from major health challenges. One 2012 study published in the Journal of the American Medical Association (Levy, Slade, and Kasl) shows that older people with positive attitudes about aging are 44 percent more likely to fully recover from severe disability than those who accept negative stereotypes about older people.

One of my favorite studies about the impact of belief systems on how we age was also conducted by Dr. Levy at Yale. The 2014 study, published in the journal Psychological Science, assembled 100 subjects with an average age of 81 and flashed words such as "spry" and "creative" across their computer screens at speeds too fast to allow for conscious awareness. Those exposed to positive subliminal messaging exhibited increased psychological well-being and a range of physical improvement, including better balance, that wasn't found in a control group. And that improvement continued for three weeks after the intervention ended.

Here's where it gets really interesting. The study showed that physical function improved *more* in the subjects who received positive messaging for six months than it did in similarly aged subjects who were placed on a six-month exercise regimen with no exposure to such messaging. The takeaway, of course, isn't that we should give up exercise. It's that we should exercise our attitudes as well as our bodies.

It has become increasingly clear that the most important thing we can do for ourselves and our loved ones is to change the way we think about aging. Because inside that basic belief system lies the success or failure of nearly every dream and desire that we may have. Those with a positive view of aging live longer, happier, healthier lives and recover more quickly and more fully from injury, disease and disability. Those who believe negative stereotypes of aging eventually exemplify those stereotypes.

Raising Corporate Profits by Lowering Self-esteem

Are you ageist? Before answering, consider this: Unless you've lived in a complete vacuum your entire life, it's impossible *not* to be ageist to some degree. And when those who are ageist become old themselves, their prejudice turns inward, leading to depression and a myriad of other mental and physical illnesses. Older people are often the most ageist of all because they've had a lifetime to internalize the ageist beliefs espoused by the 24/7 propaganda machine.

The Machine attacks our insecurities. Research shows that nearly 90 percent of all Americans are dissatisfied with or ashamed of some part of their bodies — and as we age, advertisers ruthlessly seize upon these insecurities. (Daniel & Bridges 2013) (UNC-*SELF* and Gender and Body Image (GABI) Studies) Women, in particular, are under constant pressure from beauty and cosmetic companies to fight the natural appearance of aging at every step.

The global anti-aging market is expected to exceed more than $216 Billion by 2021 as companies craft sophisticated marketing campaigns to make women hate their gray hairs and deepening wrinkles (Marketwatch Report, 2018) Of course, the not-so-subtle message is that old age is ugly and shameful — and must therefore be hidden or disguised. Because so much money is spent in an effort to make us feel insecure about our appearance as we age, it has become increasingly difficult for us to be happy and confident in our own skins.

Men aren't immune from the effort to raise corporate profits by lowering self-esteem. Consider the endless negative messaging regarding hair loss. Your bald spot or receding hairline will make you look old and unattractive. Women will find you unappealing, employers will shun you and you'll never play lead guitar in a rock band. You certainly can't *enjoy* your miserable existence, and it's only going to get worse unless you act now and pay us to take hair from another part of your body and transplant it into your bald spot. Once you've done that, women, jobs and rock bands will be yours for the taking.

As a bald man who somehow managed to work on-air in the television industry for decades, I've been approached several times over the years by companies offering me "an amazing opportunity" to take advantage of their hair-restoration product or services in exchange for an endorsement of some sort. When I kindly say, "thanks, but no thanks," they can't begin to understand why. How could any man be content without hair when he could have more with their assistance, at no cost?

Admittedly, when I first started losing my hair as a young man, I wasn't happy about it. But I deeply resented the fact that large companies were launching sophisticated advertising campaigns and spending hundreds of millions of dollars in an attempt to denigrate and embarrass me — along with millions of other men. The global hair transplant market alone is estimated to be worth 25 billion by 2024. (Global Market Insights

2018) I decided to never again worry about my hair loss. And I never have. It can be surprisingly easy to liberate yourself from nonsense.

The constant bombardment of negative images and cues about growing older have so thoroughly convinced us that aging is a time of loss and limitation that we create such a reality. We anticipate the presumed negative benchmarks of aging so completely that we actually manifest them. And the result is devastating on both a personal and societal level. We're literally killing ourselves with our belief systems. We're robbing ourselves of not only *years* of life, but *quality* of life. In addition, we're adding billions of dollars to our national healthcare costs.

Constant exposure to the message that older people are weak, incompetent and useless leads us to become dependent, noncontributing members of society. We become risk averse and reluctant to say "yes" to new adventures.

But what if we were able to view aging as an opportunity, not as a disease? What if we believed that it was possible to actually *gain* wisdom, strength, flexibility, muscle mass, kindness, empathy, speed, artistic ability and more as we age?

The truth is this: If we can change our belief system about growing older, we can change how we age. But how can that be accomplished? How can we disrupt the Machine before our future self-image takes control and has us on our backs, withdrawn and isolated, unhappy, unhealthy and unable to enjoy the opportunities of aging?

In a society that considers older people to be a burden, it's imperative that we become revolutionary. If we want to live the lives we're capable of — the lives we deserve and were created to live — we must make it happen. Nothing will be given to us.

That's why Growing Bolder exists. We're the agent of disruption. We're the intervention and the path forward. Growing Bolder is dedicated to proving that aging is not a degenerative disease — it's an unfolding opportunity that we should all be grateful to have, proud to achieve and eager to celebrate.

CHAPTER 5

REBRANDING AGING

——

It's Not a Disease, It's an Opportunity

> **"** *Positive images of the future are a*
> *powerful and magnetic force. They draw*
> *us on and energize us, give us courage*
> *and will to take on important initiatives.*
> *Negative images of the future also*
> *have a magnetism. They pull the spirit*
> *downward in the path of despair.*
> —WILLIAM JAMES

OUR LIVES ARE BEING DEVALUED EVERY YEAR by our culture, and society's willingness to invest in our wellbeing is gradually disappearing. I once had a 15-year-old luxury car that would one day be considered a classic. It had been exquisitely cared for and had very low mileage. I thought I would have it forever. And then one of my daughters was involved in a minor traffic accident and the car sustained minimal damage. "No problem," I thought. But the insurance company, considering only the Blue Book value of a 15-year old car, didn't want to repair it. So, they "totaled" the car and wrote me a check for its dramatically depreciated value.

We're all becoming the old and damaged classic car that has been dramatically depreciated, and society is the insurance company that wants to declare us totaled and not worth the effort or expense of repair. Our culture is ready to tow us to the scrap heap.

If you think that your healthcare payers and providers are fond of denying coverage and treatment now, just wait. An ageist culture that denies the value of older people will have no problem denying or withholding care "for the public good." Without a major cultural shift, we'll continue to dehumanize older people in order to justify dangerous ideas such as "saving our limited resources for younger people who can derive more benefit from them." This is a statement that's already shared privately in many government circles — and will likely soon be mentioned openly as public policy.

At Growing Bolder we say we're *Rebranding Aging*® because, to a large degree, the genesis of the current ageist culture was the advertising movement of the late '50s and early '60s. It was an attempt to glorify youth as a means to enhance brand awareness and capture the 78 million consumers known as baby boomers. I want to believe that it was an unforeseen consequence that deifying youth would lead to demonizing the elderly — but that's exactly what has happened, and continues to happen, over the past seven decades.

Tragically, a strategic (and highly flawed) decision to devalue older consumers has resulted in devaluing older human beings, and in the creation of an ageist culture that portrays growing older as little more than the loss of youth, devoid of any real benefits. The incessant drumbeat of our culture has become the desire, and even the need, to deny or disguise the natural aging process.

Growing Bolder is dedicated to deprogramming the world from the insidious cult of youth and destroying the propaganda machine that orchestrates its 24/7 brainwashing campaign, because we've all been deceived by our culture, misled by our media and lied to by Hollywood and Madison Avenue.

We believe our mission is critical to the future health and happiness of billions. Negative aging stereotypes are now a bona fide public health issue, because what the mind believes, the body embraces.

The widely accepted narrative of growing older is that it's little more than the toxic byproduct of youth — with older people poised on the boundary between a life worth living and one that should be sacrificed for the good of humankind. With every advancing year, society pushes us closer to the edge and encourages us to jump. We live in a culture in which aging is in danger of becoming a modern-day version of leprosy — a shameful, feared and misunderstood "disease" upon which others are appalled to look.

The results of this culture-wide ageist mindset are many, each more frightening than the last. With thousands turning

65 and 75 and 85 every day, healthcare costs are rapidly rising. When we spend down our entire life savings battling chronic illness, only then will the government begin providing nursing care. And with those costs rising as resources are dwindling, it'll be that same ageist culture deciding that we're too old for a new hip, too disabled for physical therapy, too unemployable for job training and too weak to benefit from the latest treatments or medicines.

When we lose our productivity, our culture loses its interest in us — in supporting us, in curing us and in encouraging us. Hopefully, that will change as I and others work to offer alternative narratives. But we must take control of our lives. Counting on society to help in any meaningful way is like counting on Powerball to fund our retirement.

A Critical Juncture

Growing Bolder is built on an optimistic view of the future. In fact, we often say that our products are hope, inspiration and possibility. But allow me to go to the dark side for just a moment. The first step in what could be a dystopian future of nightmarish proportions is already unfolding: the mass warehousing of poor and frail older people for whom our ageist society has little concern. Out of sight, out of mind.

There's a large and growing financial incentive for profit-driven companies that live off government reimbursements to keep the frail elderly alive, provided these companies can meet minimal government standards of care while maintaining an acceptable profit margin. As with any business, when margins shrink, costs must be cut in order to keep shareholders happy. As the population continues to age and healthcare costs continue to rise, many treatments, therapies and medicines will be routinely denied.

This denial will be justified by the ageist belief that the expenses aren't worthwhile or appropriate. Consequently, millions of our poorest seniors, with no money and no family able or willing to support them, will end up in what can only be described as government-funded elder warehouses, where they'll be drugged to keep them quiet and bedridden as they slowly decline. Our public eldercare system will soon make our prison system look like the Ritz-Carlton.

There are those who suggest, in all seriousness, that individuals with no assets and no family to support them commit a crime, because a federal prison may provide better living conditions and higher standards of healthcare than a government-funded nursing home. This is already happening in Japan where more than a quarter of its citizens are over the age of 65. According to Bloomberg Businessweek, the elderly crime rate in Japan has quadrupled over the past couple of decades. Nine out of 10 senior women behind bars are there for petty shoplifting with an alarming number admitting that they got caught on purpose because they were lonely, hungry or sick.

We live in a youth-obsessed culture. And now, we're in the early stages of a fight for the right of older people to be afforded access to resources and treatments that many will maintain should be reserved exclusively for the young. The Congressional Budget Office projects that 80 million Americans will be Medicare-eligible by 2035. And current predictions have the Social Security trust fund running out of money in 2037, if nothing is done. That same year, as many as 6,000 to 9,000 Americans will be turning 85 every day. Some people will then begin suggesting, not entirely facetiously, that we must transition to a society in which there are no elders at all. Before you laugh at that notion, consider that many already blame older people for a lack of resources and opportunities.

I'll leave it to your imagination to sort out how a future might unfold in which no one lives beyond a certain age. But there are plenty of references to just such a society in film and literature.

Those outlandish scenarios aside, we've reached a critical juncture in our evolution as a society that will, to a large degree, inform the future of aging around the world. Will we continue to view aging as a disease and not an opportunity? Will we condemn the old — and therefore our future selves, our children and our grandchildren — to a world of rapidly shrinking possibility? Will we learn to celebrate the old or will we continue to denigrate them?

So how do we go about our Growing Bolder mission: Rebranding Aging? How do we help men and women worldwide change their future self-image from one of sickness and despair to one of passion and purpose?

While the ageist propaganda machine never shuts down, we hold within ourselves the ability to disconnect from the belief system that is slowly killing us. We must recognize and acknowledge the cultural brainwashing to which we have been unknowingly subjected for decades. We must develop a resistance to future brainwashing through regular exposure to believable alternative narratives and real-life examples of ordinary people who are Growing Bolder.

We must understand that a moment at 80 or 90 or even 100 can be filled with as much possibility and potential for significance as a moment at 20 or 40. Yes, how we spend that moment will change, but its value does not. Even as we age and our bodies begin to weaken, our spirit, wisdom, creativity, curiosity, compassion, capacity to learn and capacity to experience love and joy can grow stronger.

Most of us look at life as sand through an hourglass. The less sand that remains on top, the less valuable our lives become. We must reprogram ourselves to look at the value of age as additive. The longer we live, the more valuable we become. As the wisdom and experience gained from a long life falls to the bottom of the hourglass, our lives become richer and more rewarding. We must begin looking at life as coming *to* us, not leaving us, as we grow older.

CHAPTER 6

THE AGEISM OF THE ANTI-AGEISM MOVEMENT

Dismissing the Exceptions that Disprove the Rule

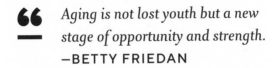

Aging is not lost youth but a new stage of opportunity and strength.
—BETTY FRIEDAN

OUR CULTURE HAS BECOME EXTREMELY EFFECTIVE at age shaming — making us fear each wrinkle and dread each year. Many age-related fears are not unfounded. If we're fortunate enough to live into old age, we'll have to deal with the physical, emotional, financial and cultural challenges of aging. Despite these challenges, we have an opportunity to age in ways that most don't realize are possible because of the ageist lies we've been told by the Machine.

Growing Bolder is about overcoming these dangerous, debilitating and life-limiting lies. It's about smashing the stereotypes of age and replacing them with relatable examples of what's possible. It's about disconnecting from ageist propaganda and deprogramming ourselves from the sophisticated brainwashing to which we've been subjected since childhood. It's about recognizing the nearly limitless opportunities of age.

Surprisingly, this information will bother some readers — including many who believe themselves to be leaders in the anti-ageism movement. Their efforts are, for the most part, well intentioned and highly admirable. But, in some instances, the efforts themselves are ageist.

There are some who see ageism in anything that celebrates what they refer to as an "idealized" vision of aging. They believe aspiring for more is an unhealthy form of age denial. The desire for vitality isn't age denial. We're not denying age when we choose to live with strength, creativity, passion and purpose. These qualities have nothing to do with age. They're about a state of mind, not a date of birth.

While it's important to be comfortable in our own skin and not ashamed to show the signs of age, it's reasonable to want to look and feel our best for as long we can. If it's possible to be fit, toned, agile, flexible and powerful as we age, then pursuing those qualities isn't *denying* aging. It's *redefining* aging.

I disagree with those who believe that celebrating exceptional older people is a form of ageism. Their accomplishments are only considered uncommon or unrealistic because we live in a culture in which the view of normal aging is wildly divergent from reality. The ever-expanding boundaries of human potential are being redrawn on a daily basis by ordinary people who have chosen to live extraordinary lives. They are the exception that disproves the rule. They are the proof that the limits of possibility have been grossly underrepresented.

Growing Bolder doesn't present an idealized vision of aging. We present a realized vision of aging to prove that many virtues associated almost exclusively with youth are not, in fact, age-related.

Many say we should never use the term *successful aging* because it turns aging into a binary event: either you're a success or you're a failure. I find this reasoning to be simplistic and absurd. In every other aspect of our lives, the definition of success is highly personal. We all understand that teaching kindergarten and shaping young minds might represent success to one person, while running a global corporation might represent success to another.

What makes a successful marriage, a successful business, a successful vacation or a successful meeting? There's no black or white. You get to choose from an infinite number of shades of gray. Likewise, you get to decide what successful aging means to you — and you're free to change or modify that vision at any time.

I'm not pushing a list of qualities that you must adopt, lifestyle changes that you must make or activities that you must pursue in order to age successfully. I'm simply providing options that are counter to the accepted aging narrative and pointing out that there are thousands of companies investing billons of dollars in an effort to make you feel inadequate, unhappy and fearful about your future.

If you choose to define successful aging as sitting on the couch and watching TV for 12 hours and then sleeping for another 12 hours because that's what you enjoy — not because you don't know that other options are possible — then do exactly that without apology.

There are some who equate aspiration and optimism when associated with aging as Pollyannaism. They believe that those who aspire for more are ignoring the realities of aging. In my experience, optimistic and aspirational people always do better, regardless of their age or condition. They're happier, healthier and better able to recover from setbacks. Optimism and aspiration are critical traits when it comes to recognizing, understanding and celebrating the beauty in aging.

Let me be absolutely clear: Struggling to hold on to the illusions of youth while avoiding the realities of aging is a no-win game. Growing Bolder is not about denying aging, defeating aging or aspiring to become ageless. We're all mortal. That means we should embrace the one inescapable fact that should inform every decision we make, every risk that we take and every thought that we think: none of us are getting out of here alive. If we're fortunate enough to live into old age, we're all going to have a period of decline. It's unfortunate that some are so focused on accepting "the realities of aging" that they can't embrace the *possibilities* of aging. Those individuals are, in my opinion, dangerous double agents of the ageist propaganda machine — promoting an anti-ageism agenda while reinforcing a life-limiting belief system.

We're not trying to make anyone feel "less than" by sharing stories of possibility. We're not peddling the false belief that all older people are capable of running marathons, climbing mountains, swing dancing and writing best-selling novels. We're not suggesting that every 90-year-old should celebrate his or her birthday with a skydive from 13,000 feet. These stories are not about the marathon that was run or the mountain that was climbed. They're about the obstacles that were overcome, the power of belief, the value of friendship and the benefit of risk-taking.

When we share the story of "Banana" George Blair barefoot waterskiing at 93 after multiple back surgeries and a near-deadly bout with pneumonia, we're not suggesting that another 93-year-old attempt such a feat. The story is not really about waterskiing. It's about passion and perseverance — and how those qualities can be applied to any life at any age.

When we share the story of 92-year-old Barbara Beskind, who goes to work in youth-obsessed Silicon Valley at world-famous design firm IDEO, we're celebrating the virtue of taking risks, the value of experience and the importance of intergenerational connection. It's not meant to be a challenge to other nonagenarians to move to California and smash the gray ceiling.

I've spent nearly 40 years as a journalist, and I take exception to those who say that age should never be used as a first-level identifier. I agree that age is not relevant to many stories, and just as including the race of an individual can be racist, including the age can be ageist. But that's what good journalism is about —understanding that each story is different and including those facts that are important and relevant to the understanding of the story.

When confronting dangerous and destructive ageist

beliefs, including age as a first-level identifier is not only appropriate, it's necessary. We can remove age from our reporting only when society fully understands that the ability to accomplish any specific task or activity is not age-related. The way to achieve that is by presenting exceptions to accepted beliefs. When we put an age next to the name of someone who is breaking an ageist stereotype, we aren't reinforcing ageism — we're fighting it.

To not report that Diana Nyad was 64 years old when she swam unaided, without a shark cage, from Cuba to the U.S. — something that no other person of any age had ever accomplished — would have been missing the story altogether. Her sole purpose in completing the 110-mile swim through treacherous waters was apparent when her first words upon emerging from the ocean in Key West were: "Never, ever give up. You're never too old to chase your dreams."

We interviewed Diana after her swim and she told us: "We're all living on a one-way street. Someday you'll get to the end, and your goal is to not look back and say, 'I should have, I could have or I wish I had.' The way to accomplish that is to never believe that age is a limitation. I truly think I'm a better athlete in my 60s than I was in my 20s."

To report that Nyad was 64, and that she implored everyone watching to chase their dreams no matter their age, was empowering and inspiring, not ageist.

Ageism is real and needs to be called out and confronted. Awareness is critical. But a powerful and transformational movement can't be based upon the Associated Press Style Guide.

For decades there has been an on-going and near frantic search for a new word to describe aging, something that makes us feel better about growing older. Companies routinely create focus groups hoping to create a description that resonates with their target markets. Aging experts write extensively about promoting a new term that will magically change everyone's perception of growing older: wisdom workers, grand elders, older adults, super agers, olders, perennials, golden agers, modern elders, third agers, boomers and countless others. It's as if we believe that when we stumble upon the right descriptive word we'll immediately feel better about ourselves, the workplace will respect us and society will appreciate our value.

This is *exactly* the problem. We have become negatively influenced by words that were never designed to be pejorative. We allow these words to impact the way we think and ultimately control what we believe. We don't need new words. We need to change or expand the definition of current words. We do that by changing the way we live. And we change the way we live by changing our belief system about what's possible.

Yes, words matter — but we can't allow ourselves to be bullied by them. We can't let someone calling us *old* or *senior* or *elderly* cause us to embrace the negative traits wrongly associated with those words. And we shouldn't be fooled into thinking that a new word will magically transform our later decades.

We need leaders not wordsmiths. We need to recapture some of the zeitgeist of the 1960s to end the growing age apartheid that threatens our future. We need serious thought leadership from some agitated alpha dogs. We have plenty of rebels without a cause. Maybe they should take on this cause.

The reason many big dogs are slow to bark is that they don't feel the bite of ageism. They don't understand the pain of indifference and the fear of neglect. Money and stature have always insulated the few from the plight of the many. That's how the world works.

We need strong individual leaders because, for the most part, our advocacy groups are struggling to stay alive. Do the Gray Panthers still exist? The Panthers are not the only endangered species. Most Elks, Eagles, Moose and Lions groups are also experiencing rapidly declining membership. So are Shriners, Jaycees, Masons and Kiwanis. They struggle to survive largely because boomers tend to reject the organizations of their parents. We like to do our own thing. Yes, I know that AARP has 37 million members but when was the last time you went to an AARP meeting? You join to get the discounts, not to change the world.

I hang out with and work with an intergenerational group of friends and colleagues. I have never known anyone who looks forward to joining AARP when they turn 50, and I have never once heard anyone mention AARP in any serious context. Ask 100 people what it means to say, "I'm an AARP member," and I'll wager that 95 of the answers would be, "That I'm getting old."

Even with an annual marketing budget approaching $350 million, AARP has failed to change the perception of its own brand. To many, joining AARP is the equivalent of giving up. It's no wonder that our culture is so ageist — and our personal belief systems so flawed — when the primary benefit of joining the "world's largest and most powerful senior advocacy group" is to be constantly marketed to by insurance companies or a 15 percent discount at Denny's when you flash a card that you're embarrassed to carry.

It's time for us to prove that middle age is not the age of indifference. If we don't have an interest in helping change the world in our 50s and 60s, we certainly won't have the power to do it in our 70s and 80s. In truth, we don't have to join groups to make a difference. We only need strong leadership and a willingness to show up at the polls. We have the votes. We just need the voices.

CHAPTER 7

SOMEONE LIKE ME

The Power of Example and the Magic of Personal Transformation

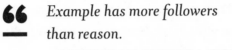 *Example has more followers than reason.*
—CHRISTIAN NESTELL BOVEE

ALTHOUGH MANY THOUGHT IT WASN'T humanly possible, Roger Bannister knew in 1954 that he could break the four-minute barrier in the mile run. Once he actually did it, the floodgates of sub-fours burst wide open. The current world record is 3:43.

The ice skating world was stunned in 1948 when Dick Button landed a double jump (two complete rotations) in competition. Today, 12-year-olds land triples and quads, which are all but required to compete internationally.

South Korean Se-ri Pak joined the LPGA tour in 1998. As a 20-year-old rookie, with her entire nation watching on television, Pak became the youngest-ever U.S. Women's Open Champion. Today, there are nearly 50 Korean-born members of the LPGA, including 5 of the top 10 players in the world. Nearly every athlete on that list says she watched Pak win the U.S. Open in 1998 and realized in that moment that it was an achievable option for her.

Once one example is shown, the limits of possibility change and belief systems are adjusted. Seeing "someone like me" living or performing in the way that we aspire to live or perform is the most powerful deprogramming tool that exists. It instantly reveals the lie, interrupts the Machine, cuts through the propaganda and can transform a life.

I can tell you that getting your first book published at age 96 is possible, but those are only words until I introduce you to Harry Bernstein, who began writing at age 93 as a form of therapy after his wife died. Harry simply wanted to record his memories of their time together, but he enjoyed the process of writing so much that what began as a tribute to his wife grew into a searing memoir about growing up Jewish in a violently anti-Semitic town in northern England. "The Invisible Wall: A

Love Story That Broke Barriers" was published when Harry was 96 and earned critical praise for its "understated poignancy and spare, weighty prose." Harry wrote two more published books before he died at age 101. He called his 90s the greatest decade of his life, saying, "The older I get, the more alive those years have become."

Simply telling you that you can become an accomplished painter in your 90s — even if you've never touched a canvas — won't overcome decades of brainwashing. But sharing the story of someone like Frieda LeFeber, who never picked up a brush until she was 76 and had her first solo show at a major gallery at age 99, is propaganda machine kryptonite.

James Aruda Henry, a retired lobsterman, had to quit school in the third grade to take odd jobs. He remained illiterate until he was 92. That's when he heard about George Dawson, a son of slaves who learned to read at age 98 and wrote a book, "Life Is So Good," at age 101. "If he can do it, I'm going to try," James said. "And that's when I started to learn."

At 92, James learned to write his name for the first time. He then began learning the ABCs and reading children's books. Inspired by George Dawson's example, James became a first-time author — writing and publishing his autobiography, "In a Fisherman's Language," at age 98 — all because of the example of "someone like me."

100 Years and 100 Meters

My favorite example demonstrating the power of "someone like me" is the story of Ida Keeling, Ella Mae Colbert and Julia Hawkins.

Ida became despondent in her late 60s following the murder of both her sons. Her daughter, fearing for Ida's mental health, suggested that they begin walking together. Their daily walk became a jog, and then a run. Running not only saved Ida's life — it soon defined it.

Just four days before her 101st birthday, Ida lined up to compete at the Penn Relays in a special mixed-masters (men and women) 100-meter dash for runners 80 and older. With more than 40,000 spectators on their feet and a worldwide television audience tuning in, she set a new women's world record in the 100-104 age group, finishing in 1 minute and 17.33 seconds.

"Thank God that I can still run," the great-great-grandmother from New York City told Growing Bolder, standing at four and a half feet tall. "I'm very happy to hear that I can inspire others. It makes me feel even greater than my height."

The video of Ida's run went viral, and it didn't take long for 100-year-old Ella Mae Colbert to hear about it and to become inspired. Within weeks of Ida's run, Ella Mae — who had never been a competitive runner — stepped onto the track behind Chesnee Middle School in South Carolina. A crowd of family, friends and a representative from Guinness World Records lined the track to cheer her on.

When the starter signaled "go," Ida took two steps and did a face plant — hitting the track and splitting her chin wide open. Certainly, everyone thought, this 100-year-old was done for the day, if not forever. Not even close. Ida asked to have her chin bandaged and within minutes she was back on the starting line ready to try again. This time she not only stayed on her feet, she beat Ida's time by more than 30 seconds. Afterward she told the crowd: "You do not stop. You'll have some trials and you'll have something that gets in your way, but you can't let it get you down. You get up and you go again."

When video of Ella Mae's run also went viral, it was seen by 101-year-old Julia Hawkins in Louisiana. Julia took up running at age 100, and when she learned that the USA Track & Field National Masters Championships would be held near her home she figured, why not? If Ella Mae and Ida did it, she should be able to as well. Running in just her second meet ever, Julia not only established a new age-group world record, she became the oldest female competitor ever in USA Track & Field history.

Suddenly, the hottest division in track and field was Women 100-104 — thanks to the power of an example from "someone like me."

Videos of all three runs have been viewed millions of times. And somewhere, another 100-year-old woman, 60-year-old couch potato or 10-year-old girl has experienced a seismic mental shift. The Machine has been interrupted and someone's internal, age-related self-image has been transformed — but not because of the results of a scientific study or the opinion of a global thought leader. The reality of possibility is only ignited when we can see ourselves in others — when "someone like me" does something that interests or inspires us. Once that occurs, it's game on.

Social Norms: The Conformity Police

Most of us have extremely limiting beliefs when it comes to growing older. That's a problem because our belief system controls our behavior and, to a large degree, determines our future. Our challenge is made more difficult by the fact we're also battling social norms, which are even more powerful than personal beliefs at shaping behavior.

Social norms are the unwritten rules about how we're

supposed to act. They're the conformity police providing constant cues for "age-appropriate" behavior. Even if we believe that aging in a certain way is possible, we likely won't act on that belief if doing so violates social norms.

Surprisingly, those who enforce social norms on older people are most often older people themselves. Peer pressure never retires nor expires; it typically grows stronger as we age. Most of our peers not only *want* us to conform, they *need* us to conform. When we don't, we challenge their belief systems and their behaviors — which makes them uncomfortable.

Growing Bolder is about breaking nearly all the social norms related to aging, because there's no such thing as age-appropriate behavior. It's about removing the accepted limits of possibility, which becomes more difficult as we grow older.

It's well-documented that when young children are told they don't have the capacity to do or understand something, they quickly internalize that belief until it becomes reality — or until a caring parent or teacher intervenes and helps them learn otherwise.

The same thing happens with older people. But it's more severe because almost no one ever intervenes to help them realize they are capable of more. That makes it nearly impossible to imagine, let alone create, a future self that diverges from the flawed and deeply internalized boundaries of possibility.

With all due respect to the study of self-image, we've found that talking about "an emotional facelift," "changing your self-image" or "reimagining who you are" can be useful in leading someone to water — but getting them to actually drink from the fountain of alternative possibility requires something more.

Stirring one's imagination through the relatable example of "someone like me" is the key to changing belief systems. It's only when we can see ourselves in others that the magic of transformation occurs.

A Natural Immunity

Of course, not every active nonagenarian and centenarian we interview was directly influenced by the example of others. There are many who seem to have some sort of natural immunity to the Machine. For the most part, these are men and women who grew up in the Great Depression or during World War II. Their childhoods were pre-television, and most of their adulthoods were pre-internet and pre–social media. The Machine wasn't up and running. Their future negative self-image wasn't being shaped by those forces.

In many cases, they grew up around grandparents who were revered. Even though their grandparents didn't engage in the active lifestyles that many elders pursue today, their acceptance by their family and the surrounding culture taught the youngsters around them to at least not fear aging.

The vast majority of us, unfortunately, have no such natural immunity. We're products of the Machine. If we want to seize the opportunities of age, we must acknowledge that we've been brainwashed — and reprogram the flawed and deadly belief system that can lead to disease, disability and morbidity.

That sounds like an immense and overwhelming task. And for many, it is. But, the truth is, it can happen very quickly and deliver amazing life-enhancing results to anyone, no matter their age or current condition. We interview people in their 90s and 100s nearly every day who are still living big, bold lives and enjoying every minute of it.

Entertainment icon Carl Reiner has written five books since

turning 90 — one book every year. Reiner told Growing Bolder: "My 90s have been my most productive decade ever. Contrary to what you may think, genes have little to do with how long you'll live. Neither of my parents lived as long as me. I think you must have something to get up for. I can't wait to turn 96 and see what interesting things I'll get to do next."

That's a stunning statement from a man who is already a decade beyond the average life expectancy. It's a statement I hear repeatedly from other men and women in their 90s.

So, how do they do it? How have they been able to escape the incessant brainwashing of our youth-obsessed culture? How have they disconnected from the ageist propaganda machine? Why are they immune to, or how have they inoculated themselves against, the decades of sophisticated brainwashing that's stealing not only years of life but quality of life from the rest of us?

At Growing Bolder, we believe the surest and quickest way to disrupt the Machine and inspire change is by sharing the stories of ordinary people living extraordinary lives and in some cases, extraordinarily long lives.

We do that by sharing the stories of the *Rock Stars of Aging* — the men and women who disprove the myth that the very old are always frail, feeble and forgetful. They are, we believe, important agents of cultural transformation, interrupting the propaganda machine and helping us escape the ageist trance that decades of brainwashing has inflicted upon us.

CHAPTER 8

ROCK STARS
OF AGING

---

*Disproving the Myth That the Very Old
are Always Frail, Feeble and Forgetful*

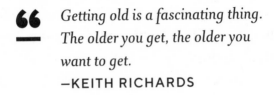

*Getting old is a fascinating thing.
The older you get, the older you
want to get.*
−KEITH RICHARDS

IN HIS BOOK "EVERYMAN," Phillip Roth, considered by many to be one of America's greatest novelists, said, "Old age isn't a battle; old age is a massacre." That's easy to say and equally easy to disprove. Growing Bolder has probably conducted more interviews with active nonagenarians and centenarians than any media organization in the world.

We've interviewed hundreds, if not thousands, of men and women in their 90s and 100s who live daily lives in which they experience great joy. They're not at war with aging, and certainly aren't the victims of an ongoing massacre.

We were there when 110-year-old Onie Ponder voted in the presidential election, when 109-year-old Ruth Hamilton became the world's oldest blogger, when Wilhelmina Hoorn danced on her 107th birthday, when Frances Shevenaugh blew out 105 candles with a single breath and when 103-year-old artist Harold Rotenberg flirted with the ladies while being honored at a major museum.

We interviewed 108-year-old Bill Hargrove between games at his local bowling alley, 103-year-old Bill Tapia between practice sessions for an upcoming ukulele concert, 96-year-old Nola Ochs after becoming the oldest person in the world to graduate college, 93-year-old Mae Laborde after moving to Hollywood to pursue her dream of becoming an actress, 97-year-old Frankie Manning after dancing with 97 different women to celebrate his birthday, 91-year-old Bernice Bates after being named the world's oldest yoga instructor and 99-year-old Orville Rogers after publishing his first book and smashing several world track and field records.

I could go on and on. If they hold a record as the world's oldest anything, chances are we've interviewed them. The world's oldest woman to reach the North Pole? Check. The world's oldest NASCAR driver? Got him. The world's oldest showgirl, oldest teacher, oldest mayor, oldest college baseball player, oldest female Olympian and oldest motivational speaker? Yes. Yes. Yes. Yes. Yes. And Yes. We've chatted with them all, and we've thoroughly enjoyed every conversation.

We never interview someone just because he or she is very old. Simply being alive at age 100 doesn't disrupt the Machine. In many ways it reinforces its poisonous propaganda. Advances in technology and medicine make it possible to live for many more years — but with little to no quality of life. Welcome to the dystopian nightmare.

However, people who are very old *and* thoroughly enjoying their lives become great inspiration for our viewers, listeners and readers — and great subjects for our ongoing "study" of the Rock Stars of Aging.

There are three major reasons why you should care a great deal about the Rock Stars of Aging:

1. They Didn't Win the Genetic Lottery

Living to an active 100 is more of a lifestyle choice than a genetic blessing. The National Institute on Aging says that longevity is 70 percent determined by lifestyle and only 30 percent determined by genes. Other studies are even more pro-lifestyle, with many now saying that only 10 percent of longevity is dependent upon your genes. The rest is about lifestyle.

2. They Make Life Worth Living

More than 90 percent of centenarians remained physically and mentally healthy well into their 90s. Many are still living at home, driving, golfing, traveling, dancing, painting, telling jokes, watching videos on the internet and listening to music on mobile devices like those their great-grandchildren use.

Most active centenarians don't suffer the chronic illnesses that are typically associated with age until shortly before dying. Gerontologists call this "compressed morbidity" (see Chapter 10). Basically, it means avoiding disease and disability until the very end, and then dying quickly. It's common for the Rocks Stars of Aging to have a great day, go to bed one night and simply not get up the next morning. Compress my morbidity, please.

3. They Live a Lifestyle That We Can Model

If active centenarians were living a lifestyle unobtainable to the rest of us, we could look on in amazement and then go about our days without aspiring to be more like them. But the facts don't lie — they prove that if we make positive lifestyle changes, we can all be more like the Rock Stars of Aging.

For some, this knowledge will be a burden. It's far easier to sit on the couch and pretend that we have no control over how we age. Just as the certain knowledge that we can lose weight through exercise and diet fails to motivate many obese people to change their lives, the knowledge that we can increase the length and quality of our lives will fail to motivate many who are unhappy, unhealthy and unwilling to believe that more is possible.

For others, this knowledge will represent a life-changing opportunity. That's because the Rock Stars of Aging are living laboratories — providing a glimpse into our possible future and a pathway to get there.

Before I reveal how active centenarians are alike, let's first consider how they're different. The Rock Stars of Aging are as diverse as any group could be. They vary widely in years of education, socioeconomic status, race, gender, religion, ethnicity, diet and genetics.

This is great news because these differences prove that there's an *opportunity* for just about anyone, living anywhere, to dramatically improve the length and quality of his or her life. While their differences provide the motivation for us to believe that living to an active 100 is a real possibility, it's their similarities that deliver a clear and proven road map to vital and active aging. Above all else, the Rock Stars of Aging prove that when it comes to longevity, it's not luck, it's lifestyle!

THE TOP TEN TRAITS SHARED BY THE ROCK STARS OF AGING

1. They Mourn and Move on

If there's a universal experience among the very old, it's continual loss. If we live long enough, we lose just about everything: our keys, driver's licenses, jobs, spouses, siblings, children, friends, libidos, hearing, vision, mobility, independence and on and on. It's one loss after another.

Eventually, the combined weight of this continual loss is too great for most to bear. Active centenarians are the exceptions. They have a selective memory. They remember the good things in life and forget the bad. They mourn and move on. They don't spend much time feeling sorry for themselves. And they don't fall into states of depression — which marks the beginning of the end for the ultra-elderly. They let go of what's lost and find joy in what remains.

Grandma Moses, who had a passion for embroidery, had to give it up at age 76 after developing a debilitating case of arthritis. Instead of feeling sorry for herself and withdrawing — as many elderly people do when they lose the ability to participate in an activity that has defined them for decades — she found a new outlet for her creativity. She took up painting because her arthritic fingers could still hold a brush. The rest is art history. She created thousands of paintings until her death at 101, and her work now hangs in museums and private collections all over the world. "Painting is not what's important," Grandma Moses said. "The important thing is just keeping busy."

2. They Have A Powerful Sense of Purpose and a Positive Attitude

The Japanese believe that everyone has an *ikigai* — a reason for being. The French call it a *raison d'être*. Call it whatever you like. Having something that makes life worth living is essential as we age.

It's common to hear about people passing away not long after retiring from a lengthy career or following the death of a spouse. It's largely because the job or the relationship provided purpose. And without purpose, the desire to live is lost. An active centenarian's purpose doesn't have to be profound. It must simply move him or her to action. Every centenarian we've interviewed says that he or she can't wait to get up each morning. Most still make daily to-do lists. Sometimes it seems that having a to-do list alone will add active and productive years to our lives. When we have nothing left to do, we have nothing left to live for.

Passion and purpose fuel the life force required for active longevity. Dr. Thomas Perls, director of the New England Centenarian Study (NECS), put it this way in an interview with Growing Bolder: "If you actually look forward to getting older, your chances of doing so are much better than if you dread aging."

Passion and purpose translate into a positive attitude. Forget the stereotype of the crotchety old man or woman screaming, "Get off my lawn!" From what we've seen, there's no rage in extreme old age. When asked what makes them angry, active centenarians invariably have the same answer: "Nothing." Life to them is a joy, not a burden. They tend to look for the good in every situation.

But they weren't necessarily always laid back. Occasionally, a daughter or granddaughter will tell us: "You should have seen her 30 years ago. She was anything but mellow!" Mellow, though, is what every active centenarian eventually becomes.

Extensive medical research confirms that anger isn't just a negative emotion; it's a disease generator that weakens the immune system and leads to high blood pressure, heart disease and other life-threatening illnesses.

Elsa Bailey celebrated her 100th birthday by skiing in Colorado. She told a local news station: "If you're positive, you can get through anything. When you think negatively, you're putting poison in your body. Just smile."

3. They Live in the Present with a Sense of Wonderment

Nearly every important philosopher in history has underscored the importance of being in the moment, of expanding the now. The Rock Stars of Aging don't live in the past, eliminating regret, and they don't worry about the future, reducing stress. They are all about the here and now — walking through life with a sense of wonder and amazement.

On one of our visits, 109-year-old Ruth Hamilton stared out the window at a white cloud in a blue sky, then talked about it nonstop for nearly 15 minutes. She wondered aloud how the cloud was formed and when it might fill with moisture and drop rain. She commented on how it was being pushed across the sky by an invisible breeze, and how it softly filtered the sunlight as it traveled. Ruth was able to look out the small window in her spartan room and endlessly amuse herself and stimulate her mind by observing phenomenon that most take for granted.

When we asked 100-year-old Roselio Muniz what he enjoyed the most about mornings, he answered: "The fresh grass and the drops of rain that look like diamonds. It's so beautiful to contemplate what the Lord has done in this world."

As soon as you believe that your life is behind you, it is. Memories are great comfort as we age, but living in the present and making new memories is an important key to longevity. Few centenarians set a goal of reaching 100. They were simply enjoying life so much that one day it happened.

4. They're Independent, Yet Social and Active in Their Communities

Most of the approximately 1,500 people recruited to the New England Centenarian Study since it began in 1995 lived independently until the age of 90. Seventy percent of centenarians still live at home, either alone or with a spouse, and 40 percent of supercentenarians (110-plus) can still look after themselves.

We spoke with 102-year-old Virgil Coffman shortly after he walked into a Chevrolet dealer in Illinois and plunked down $38,000 in cash to buy a brand-new, bright yellow Camaro. Virgil specifically wanted the special Transformers edition with the 426-horsepower engine. "Just like the one in the movie," he told us. "The ladies love it."

Rock Stars of Aging aren't hermits; almost all communicate

with a friend or family member daily. Social interaction is critical for physical wellbeing. A life of isolation isn't a pathway to an active 100 — it's a superhighway to disease and disability. Centenarians enjoy feeling they are part of their communities and enjoy helping others. Almost every centenarian we've interviewed either still does volunteer work or did until fairly recently.

At 100, Irene Johnson still volunteered for Meals on Wheels, delivering hot meals to people who were sometimes 30 years her junior but were unable to leave home. "I try not to act like I'm 100," she said. "I'd be in bed most of the time if did." Research confirms that volunteering provides as many, if not more, benefits to the volunteer as to those they serve.

5. They Keep Moving and They Don't Overeat

The notion that we can live our lives as we please and then rely on the healthcare system to fix us when we have problems is the ultimate act of personal deception. Rock Stars of Aging live surprisingly active lifestyles into their 80s and 90s. Almost all active centenarians walk daily, while many enjoy gardening. When asked to list the secrets to their longevity, nearly every centenarian we interview includes: "I keep moving."

Jean Calment, the longest-lived human on record (122 years, 164 days), took up fencing at 88 and rode her bike every day until she was 100. We interviewed Bill Hargrove, the world's oldest active bowler, when he was 106. Bill told us that he still bowled twice weekly, even with his eyesight and hearing failing, because he knew that if he *wanted* to keep moving, he *had* to keep moving.

Have you ever seen an obese centenarian? Don't bother looking because they don't exist. Obesity is a lifestyle disease that has been linked to diabetes, heart disease, dementia and some forms of cancer. Being obese in middle age roughly doubles mortality rates and is one of the most serious threats to a long life.

In Okinawa, Japan, home to the world's largest population of supercentenarians, there's a cultural habit called *hara hachi bu* that, roughly translated, means eating only until you're 80 percent full. At age 95, Donald Pellman had just broken his seventh age-group world record in track and field when he told Growing Bolder: "The most important exercise of all is pushing yourself away from the table."

6. They Don't Smoke, Drink Heavily or Take Many Medications

We've never interviewed an active centenarian who smokes. Some, though, are former smokers. According to a study at the Institute for Aging Research at the Albert Einstein College of Medicine, 77 percent of centenarians have never smoked; on average, those who did quit 41 years ago.

The CDC's National Center for Chronic Disease Prevention and Health Promotion found that cigarette smoke contains more than 4,800 chemicals, 69 of which are known to cause cancer. According to the American Cancer Society, smoking shortens life by at least 13 years. Plus, the chronic diseases caused by smoking seriously impact smokers before the habit finally kills them.

Most active centenarians are non-drinkers and none are heavy drinkers. But a few that we've interviewed credit their longevity to a regular glass of wine, a bit of brandy or an occasional shot of whiskey.

Active centenarians aren't hypochondriacs. Ask most elderly

people how they're doing and they'll answer with a long list of ailments. Ask a Rock Star of Aging and you'll get a description of how busy he or she is.

Trent Lane continued to live alone, piloting his plane, chopping wood on his farm and breaking world track and field records until shortly before his death at age 101. When we asked Trent his secret, he answered: "Stay active mentally and physically, and stay away from all prescription drugs."

Most active centenarians take only a medication or two, plus supplements. At age 110, Onie Ponder told us: "I take two pills once a day." Helen Boardman, 108, took less than that: "I take an aspirin occasionally for hip pain. That's it."

7. They Have Few Regrets

Rock Stars of Aging don't tell stories of regret because, for the most part, they have none. They've always been in touch with what they need and were able to figure out a way to live the lives they wanted. They didn't stay in jobs they hated. They didn't remain with spouses who abused them. And they didn't remain friends with people who wanted to control them.

They found ways to live on their own terms, and as a result were mostly happy. Very few who live to an active 100 have been sentenced to extra years of misery. Beyond a certain age, miserable people die very quickly. It's really that simple. The only way to get to 100 is with a smile on your face, joy in your heart and enthusiasm in your step.

8. They're Lifelong Learners

The adage "use it or lose it" seems especially true when it comes to our brains. Rock Stars of Aging have a nearly insatiable appetite for learning, and as their eyes or ears begin to fail

— which is inevitable — they don't give up their desire to learn. They fight to make whatever accommodations are necessary so that they can continue stimulating their minds and feeding their appetites for knowledge. If they can no longer read, they receive mental stimulation from audio books, listening to the radio or playing video games.

At age 101, Roselio Muniz still reads every day. "This is my favorite thing to do," he told us. "Read and read and read and read." He especially loves to conduct research on his computer. "He's waiting for me every day when I come home from work," his daughter, Millie, told us. "He has a list of things he can't wait to share. Today he said, 'Guess what I discovered? There is a planet that is made just of diamonds! Can you imagine?'"

9. They're Kind, Empathetic and Spiritual

With respect to Billy Joel, it isn't true that "only the good die young." Only the really good get to become Rock Stars of Aging.

Being self-centered might get you to 80 or 90, but it won't get you to an active 100. Active centenarians are kind and compassionate. They worry more about others than about themselves. When asked about the principles by which they live their lives, the most common response they give is: "I believe in the Golden Rule."

Wouldn't it be disappointing if only cruel, narcissistic con artists lived to be very old? There's some karmic satisfaction in the knowledge that doing the right thing is a proven pathway to active longevity.

We've never met a centenarian atheist, but we've interviewed many centenarians who attribute their longevity exclusively to faith. Most centenarians attend a church, synagogue or mosque regularly and pray daily. Faith provides relief from stress by appealing to a higher power. It also provides social connection to a community of believers. "I do a lot of praying," 109-year-old Ruth Hamilton told us. "I don't know where Heaven is, but there's something good about praying. Life is a wonderful thing if you know God. If you don't have God, you've got nothing." When we asked painter Harold Rotenberg the secret to living to 104, he snapped: "Faith in God. Don't forget it."

10. They Avoid Debt and Leverage the Health-Wealth Connection

Sixty-seven percent of centenarians have incomes below the poverty line. Although they're poor, they perceive themselves as better off than their bank balances would suggest. It's been said that not wanting something is the same as having it without all the hassles — and that's very much the centenarian lifestyle. They don't feel poor because they want for very little.

Financial planners now call longevity the biggest risk to our future because almost no one plans to live to 100 — and that includes centenarians. They've been able to avoid the tragic scenario of running out of money before running out of time by remaining relatively healthy and debt free.

At age 90, Ann Kahl lives on a Social Security check and enjoys an active social life. "How much supplemental health insurance do you have beyond Medicare?" I asked. Her reply: "Zero. My health insurance is on my feet. It's my running shoes."

"What are your total healthcare expenditures in the past three years?" I asked. Her reply: "Zero."

"How many prescription medications are you on?" I asked. Her reply: "Zero." Ann, like most Rock Stars of Aging, is successfully leveraging the Health-Wealth Connection, the foundation of all successful aging, by making healthy lifestyle choices (see Chapter 13).

There are no active centenarians in perfect health. But they teach us that we can control chronic conditions to the extent that even with heart disease, diabetes and high blood pressure we can reach 100 in a physical, mental and financial condition that allows us to enjoy it.

The takeaway from our many interviews with The Rock Stars of Aging is that most aren't genetically predestined to longevity and none, even the well-to-do, were able to purchase extra years. They're simple, humble people of varying races, religions and nationalities who teach us that everything we do today will influence the quality of life that we'll lead in the future. Or, as Dr. Perls told us: "Centenarians disprove the perception that 'the older you get, the sicker you get.' They teach us that the older you get, the healthier you've been."

CHAPTER 9

DESTROYING THE IDEOLOGY OF DECLINE

———

The Truth About Vigorous Exercise

66
———
Aging happy and well, instead of sad and sick, is at least under some personal control. We have considerable control over our weight, our exercise, our education, and our abuse of cigarettes and alcohol. ... A successful old age may lie not so much in our stars and genes as in ourselves.
—GEORGE E. VAILLANT

IF WE'RE GOING TO DEFEAT THE Machine and deprogram ourselves from the insidious cult of youth, we must first destroy the ideology of decline. We must understand that many of the diseases and chronic conditions associated with age actually have very little to do with age. They begin in our youth or early adulthood due to poor lifestyle choices and don't reveal themselves until later in life. The human body is amazingly resilient and can withstand an enormous amount of abuse. But years of poor diet, lack of sleep, insufficient exercise, a toxic environment and constant stress eventually take a toll.

Chronic illness, the true epidemic of our time, eventually robs us of our health and then our life savings. We're now spending 80 percent of every healthcare dollar — more than $3 trillion a year — on preventable chronic illness. With healthcare costs rising rapidly, we have a responsibility to ourselves, our families, our communities and our society to proactively minimize the amount of care we'll need as we age.

Healthcare must be viewed as an individual act, not as a service received. Like it or not, the responsibility has shifted to the individual — which is exactly where it belongs. The healthcare paradigm moving forward is self-care, with the patient at the center of the system and providers delivering support. Yes, we'll all require medication, rehabilitation, counseling and consultation from many different experts. But the day-to-day responsibility for our overall wellbeing begins and ends with each of us.

This is a responsibility that far too few are willing to accept if it involves much more than taking pills. We're hoping that a fountain of youth will soon be discovered, instantly handing us that for which we're unwilling to work. The remote prospect that some miracle drug or quick-fix genetic intervention will be developed is enough to keep many on the couch, unwilling to accept the fact that there is not (and never will be) a shortcut to health and wellbeing.

That's a fact worth repeating: There's no shortcut to health and wellbeing and there never will be. The advanced surgeries, therapies, medications and genetic tune-ups will never work to their full potential without active participation from the patient.

We shouldn't fool ourselves into thinking that we're "maintaining," because we're not. Maintaining is an illusion. We're either getting better or we're getting worse. We're moving slowly in one direction or the other, and that direction will gain momentum. The couch has momentum. Jogging has momentum. Laziness has momentum. Enthusiasm has momentum. The more you do something, good or bad, the easier it is to do and the harder it is to turn away from.

The Closest Thing to a Fountain of Youth

Unfortunately for those looking for a quick fix, science has determined that the closest thing to an actual fountain of youth is vigorous physical activity — a biological imperative embedded in our DNA. From the first days of human life on this planet, we were constantly on the move, searching for food and shelter while avoiding predators. The day you stopped moving is the day you began dying — the day the tribe left you behind.

This basic biological need for movement is still with us. Movement is what makes the remarkable symphony that is the human body function properly. Vigorous activity sends a message to every cell in our bodies that there's still work to be done.

Most experts break physical activity into three categories:

low-intensity, moderate-intensity, and high intensity or vigorous exercise. Exercise physiologists measure the intensity of activity in metabolic equivalents, or METs. One MET is defined as the energy that it takes to sit quietly. Low intensity exercise burns 1-2 METs and includes activities like walking, fishing, golf using a cart, boating, and light stretching.

Moderate intensity activities burn 3 to 6 METS or three to six times as much energy per minute as you do when sitting quietly. Moderate intensity exercises include brisk walking, yoga, hiking, weight training, horseback riding, canoeing and moderate dancing.

Vigorous intensity activities burn more than 6 METs and include jumping rope, running, step aerobics, swimming, carrying heavy loads, bicycling more than 10mph, playing basketball, most aerobic machines, downhill or cross-country skiing.

Others use the talk test as an easy way to differentiate between activity intensity. If you're doing a moderate intensity activity, you can carry on a conversation but you can't sing. In vigorous intensity activity, you can't say more than a few words without pausing for a breath.

Still others gauge exercise intensity by heart rate, the higher your heart rate, the higher the exercise intensity. To gauge exercise intensity using heart rate you need to know you maximum heart rate (MHR) which you can estimate by subtracting your age for 222 — so a 50-year-old has a MHR of 170. Low-intensity exercise gets you to about 40 to 50 percent of your MHR. During moderate-intensity exercise, you're at 50 to 70 percent of your MHR. A high-intensity or vigorous workout reaches 70 to 85 percent of your MHR.

Despite the incontrovertible proof of the many health benefits of exercise, most of us remain unwilling to make even modest lifestyle changes. U.S. Department of Health and Human Services figures show that 35 percent of adults don't exercise at all, while only 17 percent of men and 13 percent of women over the age of 65 are sufficiently active. The unavoidable result: 70 percent of Americans are overweight or obese. Heart disease, America's number one killer, claims one out of every three lives. Half of all adults in this country are diabetic or pre-diabetic.

Exercise never ceases to be a requirement for wellbeing. It's potent medicine that is effective, free and without harmful side effects. So, why don't more of us take this powerful medicine? Why do we ignore the fact that the average prescription drug lists 100 potential side effects, with some warning of as many as 525 potential adverse reactions?

The answer, of course, is misinformation, big money and the Machine. There are some who say that encouraging people to exercise on a regular basis is a draconian prescription. We have gotten so far away from what we are designed to do, from what we need to do, that exercise is considered cruel and extreme.

Far too many doctors prescribe medication before lifestyle modification, and far too many patients happily take those prescriptions, encouraged by ceaseless advertising campaigns from massive pharmaceutical companies. Pharma is now the seventh-largest ad category in the U.S., with nearly $7 billion a year spent on direct-to-consumer (DTC) advertising — 64 percent more than five years ago. Only two countries in the world permit DTC drug ads: the U.S. and New Zealand. These are the only two countries in which consumers are allowed to be seduced by sophisticated ads offering quick fixes in the form of expensive and potentially dangerous drugs.

We've all seen the TV commercials in which happy actors appear to finally enjoy life after asking their doctors about well-advertised prescription drugs. The actors, their ailments cured, blissfully work in gardens or walk along beaches. Concurrently, over the sound of pleasing music, an announcer casually mentions possible side effects, such as addiction, coma, hallucinations, seizures, strokes, sudden death, suicidal thoughts, liver failure, memory loss, uncontrolled movements, sexual dysfunction, bladder cancer, heart attack, impaired thinking, severe bleeding and many more gruesome outcomes. It's like a *Saturday Night Live* skit, except that it isn't.

The litany of potential disasters concludes with: "Ask your doctor if this drug is right for you." What they don't say is that the pharmaceutical industry is not only spending $7 billion a year marketing directly to consumers, it's spending another $30 billion marketing directly to physicians and other health-care professionals. They want to ensure that we ask the question — and that our doctors answer it in a way that boosts the bottom line.

I'm not suggesting that all prescription drug use is unwarranted or unhelpful. I am suggesting that free and regular vigorous exercise will produce better results — with no side effects — than the majority of expensive and toxic prescription medications.

The main reason that so many of us ignore the health benefits of exercise is that its active ingredients are getting our asses off the couch and working out. In our quick-fix society, that's a price too few are willing to pay.

One of the most destructive ageist myths perpetuated by the Machine is the belief that we'll inevitably lose flexibility, muscle mass, bone density and cardiovascular fitness as we age. Many of the studies that perpetuated this flawed conclusion, it turns out, were conducted using groups of sedentary adults — couch potatoes. The explosion in masters sports has provided an entirely new group of test subjects. And what we're learning is mind-blowing: Performance loss is mainly due to an inactive lifestyle, not biological aging. In other words, physical decline isn't a given. Actually, in many cases we can get faster, stronger and more flexible as we age. The deciding factor is regular vigorous exercise.

Without exercise, we lose 15 percent of our muscle mass between the ages of 50 and 70. After that, it jumps to 30 percent per decade. As we lose muscle mass, we gain fat and our basal metabolic rate (BMR) declines. Our BMR is the amount of energy that our bodies expend at rest, and it accounts for 50 to 70 percent of the energy we use each day. According to the American Council on Exercise, after age 45 our BMR decreases by up to 10 percent per decade. Less muscle mass and more fat, combined with a decreasing BMR, causes blood sugar levels to rise. We become increasingly vulnerable to multiple diseases and chronic illnesses.

Loss of muscle mass means loss of support for bones and joints, making falls and breaks more common. Loss of muscle mass also accelerates the normal decline in aerobic capacity — the body's ability to process oxygen. By some estimates, aerobic capacity for the average, non-active 65-year-old is only 60 percent of what it had been in youth.

It's a cascading effect that starts with a sedentary lifestyle. It leads to a nursing home, a hospital bed and ultimately to a pine box.

"You could make the case that aging starts in muscle," said

Simon Melov, a professor at the Buck Institute for Research on Aging. If that's the case, then building muscle later in life disrupts the Machine and slows the biological clock. That notion is supported by a group of Norwegian researchers who used data from multiple studies to create a calculator that estimates "fitness age." The calculator was used in a study of more than 4,000 participants at the National Senior Games. Although the average chronological age of participants was 68, their average fitness age was just 45. This is significant, because fitness age has been proven to be a better predictor of how many years we have left than chronological age.

Older people aren't the ones who should stop exercising vigorously. They're the ones who most need to start. Vigorous exercise helps keeps us alive and dramatically improves our quality of life.

Between 2006 and 2014, Australian researchers studied more than 200,000 adults, ages 45 through 75, to determine how exercise levels impact mortality. Participants were split into three groups: those who did only moderate activity, those who did some vigorous activity and those whose workouts included vigorous activity at least 30 percent of the time. The results, published in JAMA Internal Medicine, show that participants who engaged in some vigorous activity had a 9 percent decreased risk of mortality compared to moderate exercisers. And those who did the most vigorous activity had a 13 percent lower risk of mortality compared to moderate exercisers.

Vigorous exercise has been proven to be more effective than medication for many chronic health conditions. Among its benefits are enhanced cardio-respiratory and skeletal muscle function. Vigorous exercise also leads to increased levels of high-density lipoprotein cholesterol (the "good" cholesterol) and improved blood pressure. Add to the list increased bone density, more effective weight control and reduced inflammation, as well as decreased need for insulin and improved glucose tolerance. The list goes on. No matter what ails you, vigorous exercise is likely the most effective treatment available — and its side effects include more energy, better sleep and permanent weight loss.

If this sounds contrary to what we've been told, it's because the Machine has led us to believe that vigorous exercise is only for athletes — and younger athletes at that. We've been programmed to believe that vigorous activity is a heart attack waiting to happen, when in fact research reveals that it dramatically reduces the risk of a heart attack and nearly every other disease.

"There's never an age or skill level at which you can't change your fitness," said Dr. Vonda Wright, an internationally recognized authority on active aging and mortality. "When the variables of disuse, atrophy and sedentary living are removed from the aging picture, we're capable of high-level performance until our mid-70s. Does this mean that as an aging population we expect too little of ourselves, and that we're satisfied to grow older the way our parents did? My contention, as a surgeon and researcher out to change the way we age in this country, is that much of the disease and frailty we witness before our mid-70s is due to sedentary living — not aging alone."

We're beginning to better understand the impact of vigorous exercise at a cellular level. One of its many benefits is an increase in capillary density. Capillaries are the smallest of the body's blood vessels — the end of the line in an elaborate vascular network. Only one cell thick, capillaries are where the real action takes place, transferring oxygen and other nutri-

ents from the bloodstream to tissues, and collecting and haul-
ing away carbon dioxide and other waste materials.

Capillary density and capillary function both decline with
age. But both effects respond positively to vigorous exercise.
Multiple studies, including a 2009 study at Duke University,
have confirmed that vigorous exercise leads to significant
increases in capillary density, improving the body's capacity to
perform important work at a cellular level.

Capillary development is important in every part of the body,
but particularly in the brain, which literally swims in a pool of
blood. Even though the brain represents only 2 percent of the
body by weight, it consumes 20 percent of the body's oxygen
supply. Capillaries are how the brain receives the oxygen and
nutrients necessary to do its work.

Recent research reveals that the increase in capillary density
resulting from vigorous exercise occurs throughout the body,
including the brain. People who have engaged in regular, vigorous exercise over an extended period of time have substantially
more small blood vessels in their brains than people who have
been relatively inactive. This dramatically increases the body's
ability to deliver nutrients to the brain and remove toxins. This
is one very compelling explanation for how and why vigorous
exercise helps prevents cognitive decline.

Improved capillary density also leads to a dramatic increase in
mitochondria — the energy-producing structures within our
cells. Mitochondria transform the energy from food into the
cellular energy that powers the body. More mitochondria mean
more energy, more stamina and faster recovery. Unfortunately,
mitochondria also decrease with age and lack of physical activity. But guess who can make more mitochondria? You can!
Vigorous exercise is a mitochondria-generating machine.

Exercise has also been proven to protect the mind by promoting the formation of neurons in the hippocampus, a part of the brain associated with memory. The hippocampus shrinks in the very old, leading to impaired memory and increased risk for dementia. Vigorous exercise not only prevents hippocampus shrinkage, it can actually lead to an increase in its size.

A study of healthy adults age 65 and older at the University of Kansas Medical Center was designed to determine the ideal amount of exercise necessary to measurably benefit the brain. "Basically, the more exercise you did, the more benefit to the brain you saw," said Dr. Jeffrey Burns, co-director of the university's Alzheimer's Disease Center. "Any aerobic exercise was good. And more was better."

The study also indicated that the intensity of exercise appeared to matter more than the duration. "For improved brain function, the results suggest that it's not enough just to exercise more," added Dr. Eric Vidoni. "You have to do it in a way that bumps up your overall fitness level."

We recorded one of the last interviews with fitness guru Jack LaLanne before he died at age 96. Jack was a pioneer, and universally considered to be the Father of Fitness. His many accomplishments include opening the first commercial gym in 1936, producing and hosting the world's first fitness show on TV and inventing the jumping jack.

Jack was the first to advocate that athletes work out with weights. "Back then, people thought that lifting weights would prevent athletes from being able to perform with speed and agility," he said. That notion is laughable today. It would be difficult, if not impossible, to find a single professional athlete in any sport — football, basketball, baseball, golf, track and field, swimming or hockey — who doesn't engage in some form of resistance training.

Jack was also the first to advocate that women work out with weights. "Everyone thought that women weren't physically able to lift weights," he said. "Can you believe that? They thought I was crazy for even suggesting it!"

Jack also encouraged the elderly to work out with weights long before any research had been conducted on the subject. The American College of Sports Medicine now maintains that people well into their 90s can achieve significant benefits from lifting weights — and the results are almost immediate. A group of nursing home residents ranging in age from 87 to 96 improved their muscle strength by almost 180 percent after just eight weeks of weightlifting. A study at Tufts University found that older women who lifted weights for a year improved their balance by 14 percent, while a control group that didn't lift weights suffered a 9 percent decline in balance in the same period of time.

Weightlifting — or any form of resistance training — slows the loss of hormones, stimulates the natural production of growth hormones, lowers blood pressure, increases metabolism, improves mobility, provides relief from arthritis and increases bone density and muscle mass. Studies show that weightlifters have a 41 percent lower risk of cardiac death and a 19 percent reduced risk of dying from cancer.

Despite its many life-enhancing and life-extending benefits, only about 9 percent of older adults are involved in resistance training at least twice weekly. With proper supervision, even the very old can benefit from resistance training. And we'll soon laugh at the notion that seniors shouldn't lift weights just as readily as we laughed at the notion that athletes or women shouldn't do so.

Unfortunately, much of the fitness industry continues to view the world through the socially accepted prism of ageism, grossly underestimating what older adults are capable of and widely misrepresenting fitness as six-pack abs and bikini bodies. This is not only ageist, it's very poor business. To almost everyone over 40 or 50, fitness means health and wellbeing, energy and stamina, stability and movement — the qualities that lead to active longevity. Fitness is the fuel that powers experience and lowers healthcare costs.

As we age, fitness becomes less about what we look like and more about what we're capable of. One segment of the fitness industry that gets it is called "functional fitness." The overarching goal of functional fitness is to help maintain our independence for as long as possible. It does that by improving our strength, flexibility, range of motion and mobility. Functional fitness makes everyday activities easier, thereby reducing the likelihood of falls — the leading cause of fatal and nonfatal injuries for seniors.

Functional fitness borrows liberally from yoga, Pilates, Tai Chi, dance and physical therapy. It has been described as training for life, not training for an event. While traditional weight-lifting — especially machine-based weight training — isolates muscles to work independently, functional fitness exercises multiple muscle groups and multiple joints at the same time, emphasizing core stability and creating synergy throughout the body.

Always check with your doctor before starting a new exercise program. Your doctor may want to run a few tests to make sure that vigorous exercise and resistance training won't cause a dangerous rise in your blood pressure. Fortunately, almost everyone with high blood pressure can safely enjoy the benefits of strength training.

Once you get the go-ahead, find a trainer who specializes in functional fitness. And as you begin to work out, make certain that your belief system supports your efforts. After all, perceptions drive outcomes. Your beliefs, to a large degree, will determine the effectiveness of your workouts.

This is the most important and powerful concept that we must embrace to change the trajectory of our lives as we grow older. Our belief system is either the cage that confines us or the pathway to health, happiness, vitality, passion and purpose.

Unfortunately, changing belief systems and behaviors is more difficult than ever because the internet has become the most powerful and persuasive belief reinforcer in history. You can quickly find an "expert opinion" to support any outrageous, health-destroying behavior. Do a Google search for "the amazing health benefits of Coca Cola" or "why red meat is an important part of every diet" and you'll see what I mean.

The internet actively reinforces existing biases. And if we're not careful, we wind up in a closed feedback loop where validation is never more than a few keystrokes away. We live in a world where beliefs are not necessarily the result of rational, objective analysis. For many, an unattributed statistic or a quote from an "expert," especially someone with "Dr." in front of his or her name, is all that's needed to reaffirm erroneous beliefs about diet and exercise — even when credible science and nonbiased researchers conclusively prove otherwise.

Confirmation bias has become a powerful marketing tool of the Machine. Increasingly, we no longer need to search for information that confirms our bias — it finds us. Our online behavior is aggressively tracked, and content is dynamically curated to fit our preferences, interests and predispositions.

Here is the Growing Bolder truth about exercise: any exercise is better than none. But if you really want to pursue active longevity, vigorous exercise is what you need. You can dramatically attenuate the negative effects of age, and in some cases even reverse them. But it takes a commitment to a regular program of vigorous activity that includes stretching, load-bearing exercise and cardiovascular fitness.

If you *want* to keep moving, you *have* to keep moving. That's aging in a nutshell. Vigorous exercise is not only the proven pathway to a longer, more active life, it's also the proven pathway to compressed morbidity.

CHAPTER 10

COMPRESSED MORBIDITY

Live Long, Die Fast

> 66 *Why be saddled with this thing called life expectancy? Of what relevance to an individual is such a statistic? Am I to concern myself with an allotment of days I never had and was never promised? Must I check off each day of my life as if I am subtracting from this imaginary hoard? No, on the contrary, I will add each day of my life to my treasure of days lived. And with each day, my treasure will grow, not diminish.*
> —ROBERT BRAULT

IF WE MAKE A COMMITMENT TO ADOPTING a Growing Bolder lifestyle that includes vigorous exercise, we can dramatically increase our chances of extending the length of our lives, improving the quality of our lives and shortening the period of decline at the end of our lives. We can compress our morbidity. We can live hard and die fast. The most important consideration isn't how old we are when we die, but how long we're sick before we die.

Stanford University Professor Dr. James Fries coined the term "compressed morbidity" in 1980. Basically, it means compressing the period of disease and disability that most suffer during the final years of their lives. If the average person begins experiencing chronic illness at age 70, he or she may endure a decade of decline before dying at 80. If science and technology conspire to keep that person alive to age 90 without a corresponding increase in health span, that means two decades of disease, disability and morbidity. This is tragic on a personal level and financially devastating on a societal level.

But what if we could reduce the period of decline from two decades to two months, two weeks or even two days? Compressing morbidity increases the years of active, engaged, meaningful life and reduces the burden of healthcare to ourselves, our families and society — no matter how long we live. It's the ultimate win-win.

Compressed morbidity is sometimes referred to as "squaring the curve," a term coined by Dr. Kenneth Cooper, the man who introduced the concept of aerobics in his 1968 book titled, appropriately, "Aerobics."

"The curve" is the typical arc of overall health as we grow older. It's the steady decline in which our physical abilities slowly erode until we become bedridden, decrepit and dependent. For most inactive, overweight and undernourished Americans, this decline begins in our 40s and accelerates until the very end. If we square off the curve, we avoid years and sometimes decades of decline.

The good news is, we're on the brink of a longevity revolution thanks to advances in science, technology and healthcare. But the bad news is, we're getting sick much sooner and spending more time in states of chronic illness due to poor lifestyle choices.

One hundred years ago, infectious diseases such as tuberculosis, smallpox, diphtheria and tetanus were the primary public-health enemies. Today, we've virtually eliminated mortality from these diseases. However, preventable chronic infirmities from atherosclerosis, emphysema, diabetes, cirrhosis and osteoarthritis have taken their place.

Given the cost of treating these conditions, compressed morbidity is not just a desirable goal for individuals — it's a financial necessity for society. Americans will be turning 75 at the rate of nearly 10,000 every day in 2027. Without compressing our morbidity, we'll face much higher healthcare costs that will consume an ever-larger proportion of the national budget.

The prospect of millions of frail elderly people who require 24/7 care and can't afford it will lead to mass warehousing where "advances" in medicine and technology will conspire to keep them alive with little to no quality of life.

Dr. Ezekiel Emanuel, an oncologist and bioethicist, is among those who believe that increases in life expectancy will be accompanied by longer periods of morbidity. In other words, he's not a believer in compressed morbidity. Dr. Emanuel told us that he hopes to die at age 75. "Life is not worth living beyond that," he said. "By 75, creativity, originality and productivity are pretty much gone for the vast majority of us."

Dr. Emanuel's sad and myopic assessment of aging can only be called ageist. Tell Harold Rotenberg, who was painting highly coveted expressionistic landscapes at age 103, that the last 28 years of his life weren't worth living. Or Mae Laborde, who didn't start acting until age 93 and worked regularly until 101. Or Ruth Hamilton, who started video blogging at age 109. I could go on and on. We have interviewed hundreds of nonagenarians and centenarians who live active and richly satisfying lives before experiencing short periods of decline. Their lives burn brightly until the very end.

Ray Kurzweil, Google's director of engineering and a world-renowned futurist, sees an unprecedented longevity boom unfolding — and views it as a very good thing. Said Kurzweil: "People wax philosophically, wondering, 'Do I really want to live past 90?' I've talked to 95-year-olds who want to see 96. Those who overcome or avoid the typical infirmities of age don't wonder if they really like being alive. They most definitely want to continue living. People sometimes say that it's short lives that give meaning to life. It's actually death that's the robber of meaning."

Positive Lifestyle Modification

So, how do we do it? How do we maximize our health span and delay the onset of chronic infirmity? How do we compress our morbidity? The simple answer is PLM — positive lifestyle modification (see Chapter 13, The Health-Wealth Connection). Regular exercise, good nutrition, plenty of sleep, reducing stress and increasing social engagement have been found in countless studies to decrease blood sugar, increase muscle mass, lower blood pressure, improve cholesterol, lessen body fat and dramatically improve nearly every other accepted health status indicator.

Scientists and researchers can tell us what they think might be possible as we age. But it takes someone like Dr. Charles Eugster to prove that age is just a number and that vigorous exercise not only helps us live better; it helps us die better by compressing our morbidity.

Charles was a retired dentist who took up competitive rowing at age 63 and became the World Masters Rowing Champion. As he grew older, however, it became more difficult to find training partners. And despite an occasional workout, he gained weight and quickly lost both muscle mass and energy. At age 87, vanity got him off the couch for good. "I looked in the mirror one morning," he said. "I didn't like what I saw, so I decided to rebuild my body."

Charles hired a personal trainer and began lifting weights, eventually becoming a Masters Bodybuilding champion. In 2014, at age 95, he decided to take up running after reading an article about high-intensity interval training being good for the heart. "I wanted to show that you can start something completely new at any age," he said.

Just a year later, he obliterated the world record for the indoor 200-meter dash in the 95-99 age group, and immediately cast himself in the role of outspoken evangelist for active aging and vigorous exercise. "Old age has been reduced to suffering with chronic disease, but it doesn't have to be that way," he insisted. "Anybody that tells me that they're too old to exercise, I tell them to make an appointment at the crematorium because they won't live long."

Charles wanted to change the perception of what's possible for the ultra-elderly. He hired a publicist and began promoting himself as the fittest nonagenarian in the world. Unfortunately, he died from sudden cardiac arrest at age 97, just a couple of weeks after competing in the world championships. Of course, this ruined his business plans. But in my mind, it only strengthened his message. He not only compressed his morbidity, he eliminated it — living an active, adventurous, passionate and purposeful life until the very end. "Life really started getting better when I reached 90," he once said. "I can tell you that life is fantastic, stupendous, amazing, exciting, glorious and wonderful. My God, it's absolutely super!" He left us with his three rules for active aging:

1. **"Never retire.** Retirement is a financial disaster and a health catastrophe. We must get rid of retirement, re-educate older people so they can get new jobs and rebuild their bodies so they can start new lives.
2. **Watch your diet.** We have the bodies of hunter-gathers, and they had enormous variety in their diet. We should continue consuming naturally produced food and avoiding manufactured and processed foods.
3. **Engage in vigorous exercise.** We must train harder and work the muscles to exhaustion or failure. And we need to vary our training. Routines should be completely changed every five to six weeks. The reason there are so many injuries in sports is because of the enormous repetition; doing the same thing over and over again. The answer is to cross train for multiple sports."

Over the years, we've met many Charles Eugsters. We've also booked interviews with extremely active centenarians only to find that they've passed away before we could get together.

I'm always sad that they're gone. But I choose to look at their sudden deaths as positive examples of compressed morbidity. One day, at age 95 or 105, they were living lives of passion and purpose and anxious to share their stories. The next day, they were gone.

Sign me up for compressed morbidity.

CHAPTER 11

THE SCIENCE OF GROWING BOLDER

Proof That We Have More Control Over How We Age

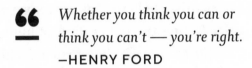

Whether you think you can or think you can't — you're right.
—HENRY FORD

LIFESPAN AND LIFE EXPECTANCY are two very different things. Life expectancy is a statistical average. It's the age to which most of us can expect to live. It accounts for those who live to be very old and those who die in childbirth. Life expectancy was very low in the Dark Ages — so many died at birth. There was also an endless list of untreatable diseases, very little medicine, no healthcare, a high likelihood of deadly accidents, infection, malnutrition and more. And, of course, no one swam laps, ran triathlons or worked out at the local gym. Life expectancy has risen dramatically over the past couple hundred years, but not because of a change in human genetics or the aging process. It has risen because of improved healthcare and better lifestyle choices. We're not changing vehicles. We're simply getting better mileage.

Lifespan is defined as the age of the oldest living individual of a species. For humans, it's 122 years, 164 days. That's how old Madame Jeanne Calment was when she died in France in August, 1997. Lifespan is closely tied to genetics, and it's believed by many that Calment got every drop out of human genetic potential. If true, that means that we all have the *potential* to live to 122 but that's about it. That's where the trail ends. Without genetic intervention, it's highly unlikely that lifespan could increase as dramatically as life expectancy has.

The Crazy Quest for Immortality

Let's get back to genetics for a moment, because an increasing number of scientists believe that in fact we will soon be able to dramatically alter the upper limit of human lifespan. "Researchers are closer than ever before to unlocking the door to life extension," says Dan Perry, executive director of the Alliance for Aging Research in Washington, D.C. "With genetic intervention, expect to see many more people — half the population — with life expectancy to 100."

And that's the conservative view. An increasing number of researchers are excited about something called "longevity escape velocity," a hypothetical situation in which for every year that we are alive science will be able to extend our life for at least another year. The concept was first publicly proposed by David Gobel, co-founder of the Methuselah Foundation, a non-profit dedicated to extending the healthy human lifespan through tissue engineering and regenerative medicine therapies. It's been widely championed by Aubrey de Grey, a British researcher commonly referred to as the "Prophet of Immortality." He believes that the first human to live to be 1,000 years old may already be alive.

I found this notion so outlandish that we booked de Grey for an interview. The conversation was mind-blowing. He thinks of aging as a curable disease and has identified seven things (mostly toxic byproducts of metabolism) that need to be prevented in order to bioengineer a human who doesn't age. His plan involves periodic repairs using stem cells, gene therapy and other emerging technologies. This "longevity tune-up" could, he suggests, add 30 years to our lifespans. During that 30-year period, new medical technologies will be developed so rapidly that we'll soon be able to get a new tune-up that will last another 30 years. And science will once again advance enough before the next "scheduled service" that we reach longevity escape velocity and death can be postponed indefinitely.

Lest you think de Grey is alone in this notion, consider that renowned futurist Ray Kurzweil, of Google, also subscribes to it. How soon might this occur? "It's likely just another 10 to 12 years before the general public will hit longevity escape velocity," he told me during an interview at the Lake Nona Impact Forum in Orlando, Florida. "The next decade will bring about a profound revolution in biotechnology with nanorobots basically finishing the job of the immune system with the ability to seek and destroy cancerous cells and repair damaged organs."

While this makes for great conversation at the dinner table, not everyone believes this is possible or even desirable. One fear of an ageless society is the rise of a gerontocratic elite that holds all of the power and controls all of the jobs. And unless age regression treatment is equally available to all, a two-tier society will quickly evolve based upon who has access to the treatment. This would become the ultimate dividing line between the haves and the have-nots in a world that already struggles with massive social inequalities.

The problem with these longevity moonshots is that they totally ignore the role of personal commitment. There is no silver bullet that will deliver a life of vitality for 100, 150 or 500 years. No matter what interventions might be cooked up they will be subservient to this one incontrovertible fact of life: If you want to keep moving, you have to keep moving. In the absence of mobility, nothing will keep us alive with a quality of life that makes living worthwhile. And mobility doesn't come in a pill or a shot or even genetic intervention. It comes from desire, determination and dedication.

The Excuse

When faced with the knowledge that it's possible to live an active life into our 90s and 100s and that compressed morbidity is an achievable goal, many people will still default to the same excuse: "Yeah, but I've got bad genes."

That excuse is just another lie perpetuated by the Machine.

Multiple research studies have proven that active longevity is only 25 percent genes and 75 percent lifestyle choices. And as we get older, genes become less of a factor in our overall health and wellbeing.

One of the major reasons that our lifestyle is more important than our genes is that our lifestyle actually has a high degree of control over our genes. We may be genetically predisposed to breast cancer, Alzheimer's disease, obesity, cardiac disease, osteoporosis, alcoholism or dozens of other diseases. But whether or not the genes responsible for these conditions express themselves is determined by our lifestyle choices: our thoughts, attitudes, perceptions and actions.

Stated another way, genes might put a loaded gun in our hand — but it's our lifestyle that pulls the trigger.

Epigenetics

The science of epigenetics is the study of how genes can be controlled by factors other than an individual's DNA. Epigenetics proves that external factors switch genes on and off, and that our DNA is not an immutable fact of our biology but is highly responsive to lifestyle choices and environmental influences.

Dr. Michael Bauerschmidt, an expert on the human genome, said, "How we approach life, our attitude toward life, affects how our genes express themselves." Dr. David Heber of the UCLA Center for Human Nutrition agrees: "The idea that it's all in your genes is nonsense. The human genome changes only one half of one percent every million years. The obesity epidemic is only about 30 years old, so changes in genes do not explain the recent dramatic rise in obesity."

The belief that our potential for long-term health and active longevity is predetermined and all but out of our control is just another empty excuse perpetuated by an ageist culture and its constantly running propaganda machine. We're not simply victims of our heredity living out a predetermined fate. We're not helplessly waiting for science and medicine to intervene and give us hope. Hope exists, but we're the ones who must actualize it.

The foods we eat, the air we breathe, the thoughts we think, the activities in which we engage and the people with whom we associate all dramatically influence not only our overall health, but also how we age. We can literally rewrite our genetic programming.

Epigenetics proves that our lifestyle habits, including our belief systems, turn genes on and off. If we accept decades of disease and disability as a natural part of the human condition, then we'll literally reprogram our genetic code and create that biological reality for ourselves and our descendants. This is already beginning to happen. The majority of people over 65 are now living with multiple preventable chronic diseases. Life expectancy for Americans has dropped for the first time in decades. Diabetes, obesity, hypertension, arthritis and many types of cancer are all on the rise in younger people.

Practicing positive lifestyle modification today will not only improve our future health, it will make it less likely that generations to come — our children and grandchildren — will experience many illnesses.

How's that for an awesome responsibility and a lasting legacy?

Telomeres

Now, for the first time, we have incontrovertible proof

about the positive impact of lifestyle choices on how we age at the cellular level. Dr. Elizabeth Blackburn and her colleagues, Carol W. Greider and Jack W. Szostak, won the Nobel Prize in Physiology or Medicine in 2009 for discovering telomerase — an enzyme that plays a key role in cellular aging.

Telomerase repairs telomeres — the caps on the ends of our chromosomes that protect our DNA and maintain accurate cell division. Telomeres have been called our biological clock because they determine the lifespan of cells. Dr. Blackburn, in an interview with Growing Bolder, likened telomeres to "the plastic tips on the ends of our shoe laces, which, when worn down, allow the laces to fray." Each time a cell replicates, we lose a tiny bit of our telomeres, which eventually become so short that the chromosome becomes "frayed." This damages our DNA to the extent that we can no longer make accurate copies of our cells. That, simply stated, is the beginning of the end.

Dr. Blackburn's research revealed that lifestyle choices can protect and repair telomeres, slowing their shortening. Now we know with certainty, at a cellular level, that regular exercise, reduced stress and an improved diet can slow our biological clock and shave years off the cellular aging occurring in our bodies. Her research proves that it's not just how much we move and what we eat that impacts us on a cellular level. It's also what we think — and this is where the Machine has done its most damaging work.

People who live the longest have the best attitudes about the aging process. Psychology trumps physiology almost every time.

Neurogenesis

The discovery of ongoing neurogenesis — the adult brain's

ability to generate new cells and new synaptic junctions — has proven to be one of biggest scientific breakthroughs in neuroscience over the last 30 years. This incredible morphing ability, also known as brain plasticity, enables the brain to literally rewire itself over time.

Neurogenesis is facilitated by a protein called BDNF (brain-derived neurotropic factor), which is essential for maintaining healthy neurons and creating new ones. Low levels of BDNF are found in nearly every instance of abnormal cognitive functioning, and have been directly linked to Alzheimer's disease, accelerated aging, obesity and depression.

BDNF is a good thing. You want more of it. Vigorous exercise has proven to be the fastest and most effective way to boost BDNF levels and improve learning, memory and mood. In Chapter 9, I wrote extensively about the many benefits of vigorous exercise, including capillary development and mitochondria production — both of which support neurogenesis. Recent studies confirm that those with Alzheimer's disease have advanced states of both capillary and mitochondrial dysfunction — yet another compelling reason to engage in vigorous exercise.

There are two other exciting and proven pathways to neurogenesis and brain plasticity: complex physical and mental novelty, and creative engagement.

The Power of Complex Physical and Mental Novelty

The human brain is the ultimate "use it or lose it" organ. If you want yours to keep working throughout your life span, you must continually challenge it to learn new things. You can be a whiz at advanced mathematical calculations, but learning to dance and mastering new choreography will be better for your brain than solving more differential equations.

You can be a concert pianist, but learning to golf will be better for your brain than learning a new Beethoven sonata. You can be a best-selling author, but learning to juggle or speak Italian will be better for your brain than writing another novel.

One simple yet effective way to encourage, if not force, neurogenesis is to simply begin using your opposite or non-dominant hand to hold a fork, brush your teeth, write a note or throw a ball. Think of it as cross-training for your brain. Your non-dominant hand (or foot) is linked to the non-dominant hemisphere in your brain. Using your non-dominant hand confuses your brain, which by default reduces routine movement patterns into a kind of shorthand that requires no thought. This process is a marvel of efficiency because it allows your brain to operate on a kind of autopilot. Using your opposite hand turns off this autopilot and forces your brain to better integrate its two hemispheres.

Research shows that musicians who use both hands have a 9 percent increase in the size of their corpus callosum or white matter — the part of the brain that connects the two hemispheres. Developing ambidexterity leads to more transfer between the hemispheres, increasing brain plasticity and mental dexterity and jumpstarting creativity.

The Corpus Callosum Poster Girl

Speaking of the corpus callosum, allow me to introduce you to Olga Kotelko.

Olga was an ordinary grandmother living in Vancouver when she retired from teaching in 1984 and discovered a love for athletics. She joined a slow-pitch softball team and played until she was 77. Then she became interested in track and field.

In 1999, at age 80, Olga competed in her first World Masters Track and Field Championships in England, winning six gold medals and setting two world records. By the time she reached her 90s, Olga was a globetrotting international celebrity who spent her time competing in world championships, setting nearly 40 world records, writing an autobiography and entertaining and inspiring everyone she met with her quick wit and sharp mind.

Scientists began wondering what was responsible for Olga's late-in-life success. So she agreed, at age 93, to allow researchers at the Beckman Institute for Advanced Science and Technology to take MRIs of her brain. About a month after Olga's visit, a neuroscientist by the name of Aga Burzynska started a new job at the institute. While asking about research projects that she might undertake, she learned about Olga and her recent tests.

At first glance, Dr. Burzynska didn't notice anything peculiar about Olga's brain scans. Her brain had shrunk slightly and wasn't pristine — typical for someone of advanced age. What eventually captured Dr. Burzynska's interest was the condition of Olga's corpus callosum, also known as white matter. White matter consists of axons, fibers that transfer nerve signals between the brain's two hemispheres, and myelin, a fatty substance that coats axons and increases how efficiently those nerve signals travel. There's a well-documented connection between white matter — which typically deteriorates over time — and cognitive abilities.

As we age, some axons die off and the myelin coating begins to degrade on those that remain. As a result, signal transmission from one part of the brain to another becomes less efficient, resulting in cognitive decline and decreased mobility.

Dr. Burzynska discovered an unusually large amount of healthy white matter in Olga's brain — more than in most people many decades younger.

It's now believed that Olga developed this white matter, while most her age were losing it, due to her infatuation with the most technical events in track and field. She didn't just run — she hired a world-class coach and trained religiously to compete in events such as the hammer throw, discus, shot put, high jump, hurdles, long jump and pole vault. She wanted not only to compete in these complex physical activities, but to master them. Her success in the events, and the impact of the training on her brain, adds to the growing body of evidence that complex physical activities convey far more brain benefits than less complex activities, such as walking the same path every day.

In 2014, at age 95, Olga traveled to Budapest for the World Masters Indoor Athletics Championships, where she won 10 gold medals and set 9 world records. She said goodbye to her many friends and flew home to Canada. There she continued training and finished writing her autobiography, "The O.K. Way to a Happy, Healthy Life." A few weeks later she had a brain hemorrhage, lost consciousness immediately and died within three days.

Olga's mind was razor sharp to the very end, and doctors say she endured no suffering. It was a textbook example of compressing morbidity through high levels of physical activity (see Chapter 10) and achieving extreme cognitive health through complex and novel activities.

We interviewed Olga when she was 91. In that interview, she credited constant activity for enabling her globe-trotting lifestyle and all but predicted how her life would end. "I don't intend to ever stop," she said. "I'll probably just drop on the field one day. There is no reason to stop. I love traveling. I love making new friends. Seniors set up barriers for themselves. Don't say you can't do this or that. You have to be courageous enough to break the many false barriers."

While crossword puzzles might be fun, their brain health benefits pale in comparison to complex, vigorous exercise. Bruce Grierson, author of a book on Olga, puts it this way: "For building cognition, Sudoku is a shovel and exercise is a bull-dozer."

The Power of Creative Engagement

One of the greatest gifts we possess as we age is creativity. A long-term study published in the Journal of Aging and Health examined a variety of personality traits and concluded that only creativity confers significant life-extending benefits. Subjects who demonstrated above-average creativity enjoyed a significantly lower risk of Alzheimer's disease and a 12 percent decrease in mortality over an 18-year period.

Art therapy programs that incorporate music, paint-ing, dance, writing, poetry and storytelling are revolutioniz-ing nursing care, home care and memory care programs by adding meaning, joy and a vibrant sense of wellbeing to the lives of older people. Social engagement, which nearly all these programs provide, has been found in major studies to prolong life and enhance healthy aging. Clinically, arts partici-pation has been linked to lower blood pressure, reduced levels of stress hormones and increased levels of the "happiness hormones" that are responsible for a runner's high.

In all cases, art therapy programs focus and capitalize on what remains, not on what's been lost. In that way, they're having a profoundly positive impact — not only on the lives of participants but also in destigmatizing memory loss.

The mechanisms behind the health benefits of creativity are not fully understood, but most researchers believe it's because creative thinking draws on a variety of neural networks within the brain. Creativity is, at its core, simply problem solving. Any great painter or composer will tell you that a blank canvas or blank sheet of music paper is simply a problem to be solved.

People who are more creative are better problem solvers, better at taking what is and constructing what *can be*. They're better at adapting to circumstances and dealing with functional limitations as they age. They're better able to find solutions that allow them to move forward without being trapped by the challenges of aging. This ability dramatically reduces stress, which is a powerful disease generator.

The good news is, creativity is not a rare gift or magical process that only some possess. Creativity is part of human nature and one of our most important human gifts. Anthropologists believe that man developed the ability to imagine things that didn't exist — but possibly could — about 60,000 years ago. That led to the creation of mythology, gossip and eventually storytelling.

The ability to fabricate stories and imagine alternate scenarios led directly to the rapid evolution of our brains and is responsible for all human progress. Our stories changed our brains and ultimately our realities. It's our innate creativity that separates us from all other animals.

When we were kids, we were encouraged to develop our artistic natures. Art was part of the curriculum in every school in America. We drew, danced, sang, acted, wrote poems and played musical instruments.

But at some point, if we didn't show what our teachers or parents believed to be exceptional ability, they took away our crayons so that we could get serious about the so-called "important stuff."

Fast forward 50 or 60 years and we're learning that art *is* the important stuff.

It's true that some are more easily connected to, and in touch with, their creativity than others. But for most, it's never a lightning strike of ingenuity. It's the by-product of fearlessness and persistence. It's simply taking an action and then refining and editing. It's a process that can be laborious but richly rewarding. It's something that we should find a way to incorporate into every aspect of our lives.

Creativity is a great screenwriter toiling over a single line of dialogue until it's perfect, poignant and, most of all, natural. Creativity is disguising the effort it takes to make something look easy. It's Jackson Pollock throwing and dribbling and splattering paint until it all starts to make sense — until order emerges from the chaos.

Creativity is you in your office at home, pondering solutions to a problem. It's you in the kitchen making a meal from last night's leftovers. Creativity is brainstorming. It's looking from multiple perspectives with variable resources until "suddenly" a solution appears.

Don't ever say "I'm not creative," because you are. We all are. It's important to our futures that we acknowledge this and nurture the creative spirit within us. It's not only important that we pursue our creative talents, but also that we encourage others to do the same. A single bit of encouragement can change the trajectory of one's final decades — just as it did for Frieda Lefeber.

Ageless Art

Frieda Lefeber, at age 76, had made only one painting her entire life. It was a portrait of her young daughter, finished decades ago. It was sitting in a box when a friend, who happened to be an art instructor, saw it and asked: "Who did that?" Frieda answered: "I did, 55 years ago." Her friend told Frieda that she obviously had talent.

That's all it took. In her late 70s, Frieda purchased a few supplies and enrolled in an art class at Rosemont College in Pennsylvania. After taking classes three days a week for more than a year, she submitted a portfolio of her work to the Pennsylvania Academy of the Fine Arts. But her application was rejected. Undeterred, she continued painting, applied again, and at age 79 was finally accepted.

Frieda drove herself to class four days a week for four years before becoming one of the academy's oldest graduates, at age 83. In 2015, at age 100, Frieda was honored with a one-artist, three-week gallery show at Rosemont College. The show included 24 original paintings, 19 of which were sold. Since graduating, Frieda has painted and studied in Russia, Italy, Germany, France and the U.S.

Frieda lived for decades believing that she had no creative talent before discovering in her late 70s that creativity was in her all along. But, unlike most of us, she was willing to take the risk and do the work required to develop her creativity. The rewards have added immense value to her life in her 80s, 90s and now 100s.

Even if she had never received any acclaim or sold any paintings, the personal satisfaction, social connection and mental and physical health benefits alone would have made Frieda's creative efforts worthwhile.

The science is now irrefutable. We can no longer fool ourselves. We can no longer sit on the couch and rationalize that we must accept a fate predetermined by our genes. We have the power to switch our genes on and off. We can rewire our brains. We can slow our biological clock. It all starts with positive lifestyle modification. And the most important modification that you can make is to your belief system about aging.

CHAPTER 12

PREHABILITATION

——

Leveraging Life's Ultimate No-Brainer

66
—
We forget that every good that is worth possessing must be paid for in strokes of daily effort. We postpone and postpone until those smiling possibilities are dead. By neglecting the necessary concrete labor, by sparing ourselves the little daily tax, we are positively digging the graves of our higher possibilities.
—WILLIAM JAMES

GEORGE BLAIR, AKA BANANA GEORGE, became the world's oldest barefoot water-skier in his mid-80s. And every time he skied after that, he broke his own record for the oldest person to successfully barefoot.

George called one day to tell me that he was going to attempt to barefoot water-ski one final time. We hadn't spoken in many months, and I was surprised to learn of his plans. The last time I'd called to say hello, George's wife, Joanne, told me that he was in bed with a serious case of pneumonia and couldn't move — not encouraging news about a 93-year-old who, on a good day, struggles with the pain and stiffness from six major back surgeries and a broken neck.

I questioned the sanity of attempting this feat, given his weakened condition. But George insisted that he was going to do it. And I agreed to be there with a camera crew to document what would be a new world record.

When the day arrived, I stood on the dock behind George's house in Winter Haven, Florida, as he was carefully helped out his back door. With a nurse on either side to prevent him from falling, George shuffled toward the water, each step covering only a few inches. I wondered how he was ever going to make it to the dock, let alone barefoot water-ski.

I wasn't the only one who had questioned George's decision. "I've had every one of his doctors and family members call me and tell me that this is not a good idea," said Lane Bowers, his good friend and boat driver. "But this is what he lives to do, so I'm trying to help. I'll keep him as safe as I can, but we're going to take him out there."

"Of course I'm worried," Joanne confided. "I'm worried every time he goes out on the water. But I can't stop him. Nobody can. Believe me, I've tried."

Bowers quickly pulled away from the dock. And when the boat reached speed, George stepped out of a special swing-like contraption and put his bare feet on the water's surface. He only had enough grip strength in his arthritic hands for one attempt — and the clock was ticking. He stayed up for a few seconds and then tumbled violently into the lake, disappearing underwater. A few tense moments later his head popped up and he shouted: "I'm OK!" It wasn't pretty but it was inspiring and it was a new record for the oldest person to barefoot.

Inside his home a short time later, George wanted me to see a sign hanging in his kitchen that summed up his philosophy of life. The sign simply read: "Do It." Then George said something that I'll never forget: "All of life is up and down. I don't stay down, and I don't wait for the next thing to happen. I make the next thing happen."

As we age, if we wait for the next thing to happen, either it never will or, if it does, it will more likely than not be a bad thing. If, like George, we *make* the next thing happen, more often than not, it's a good thing. That doesn't mean bad things can't or won't happen. That's life. But by taking the fight *to* life instead of simply playing defense, we can avoid many of the typical setbacks of advancing age. And when these setbacks occur, we can minimize their impact and speed our recovery.

As I drove home, I wondered what George's family and friends would have thought if he had died that day. He knew the risk that he was taking. And yet he said yes. Not only did he not die, at age 93 and despite declining health, he was visibly energized by the effort.

That was the last time I ever saw or spoke to George. He and Joanne moved to their apartment in New York City a short time later. And although George never again skied, I truly believe that his fearlessness and willingness to embrace risk on that day added years to his life by inspiring him to keep fighting, to keep believing that he had yet to exhaust every opportunity life offered.

George lived in New York City for five more years before dying peacefully at home at age 98. One of the last things that he said to me was, "I'm not growing older; I'm growing bolder. How do you like that?" I liked it a lot.

George had to overcome significant challenges throughout his life. It was his commitment to fitness and his determination to bounce back from each setback that enabled him to pursue the lifestyle he loved for decades longer than most thought possible.

Growing up during the Great Depression, George often hopped a freight train to get back and forth to college. On one trip, a gang of vagrants robbed him and tossed him off the moving train. He was seriously injured in the fall, displacing his spine and pinching a large bundle of nerves. He lived with the injury and intense pain for nearly two decades before undergoing spinal fusion surgery at age 39. While recovering in Florida, he decided to try water-skiing. At age 40, despite a large steel back brace, George discovered his unlikely passion. "It was like I was born again," he would say later.

Despite suffering five more broken backs and a broken neck, George never surrendered. He never allowed his injuries to rob him of his passion. Adversity taught him that that he could overcome all obstacles. Just as a vaccine inoculates against a virus, George's past inoculated him against the Machine and its lies.

Aging's Ultimate No-Brainer

For centuries, when an older person encountered a major physical setback, such as a heart attack or stroke, it was the beginning of the end — and the trip didn't take long. These health crises initiated what was almost always a grim decline. But a new model of aging is slowly emerging.

It's no longer our chronological age but our overall fitness level that determines both the types of interventions offered when we become ill and the extent of our recovery afterwards. A major setback need no longer signal the beginning of the end. It can be the beginning of a period of dedicated, focused recovery followed by a return to years of active and passionate living.

Dr. Robert Masson, Growing Bolder medical director and founder of the Masson Spine Institute in Orlando, Florida, is an internationally recognized surgeon specializing in spinal injury and sports spine medicine. More than two decades ago, Dr. Masson began requiring his patients, whenever possible, to prepare for the trauma of surgery by undergoing a process that he dubbed "prehabilitation."

"When surgery is indicated but not necessitated right away, we put our patients into an aggressive prehabilitation program to build up their overall strength and wellness prior to surgery," he said. "Prehabilitation minimizes the potential for functional loss during the early part of recovery and dramatically increases the chances of achieving extreme recovery. In some cases, an aggressive prehab routine even negates the need for surgery."

It's a given that we'll all encounter physical setbacks and health challenges as we age. So why shouldn't we be actively prehabilitating all the time — not just in preparation for a surgery? If you don't like the idea of regular exercise, think of it as prehabilitation. It's aging's ultimate no-brainer because it will, to a large degree, determine if our health challenges are bumps in the road or the end of our journey.

I'm continually amazed by those who characterize the pursuit of fitness and overall wellbeing after a certain age as a form of denial about the realities of the human condition. Their point is always that our life span is what it is, and that there's little that can be done to increase it. Therefore, they say, we should ignore the "mania" over lifestyle improvement and accept the "realities of growing older."

They're missing the point altogether. We don't exercise because it will help us live longer. We exercise because it makes us feel better. We exercise because it improves the quality of our lives. We exercise because it gives us energy and makes us happier. We exercise because it helps us to avoid sickness and recover from setbacks more quickly.

I recently read a book in which the author proclaims that she is "old enough to die" and has therefore decided to discontinue medical screening tests. Of course, this is her privilege. But she is denying the benefits of medical and technological advances and ignoring the new reality of human potential and extreme recovery.

I have a news flash for her. Everyone is old enough to die. It happens in the womb and to infants, toddlers, teens, young adults, middle-aged people and the very old. There are some things that we can't defeat with diet, attitude or exercise. Bad things happen every day to good people. Tragedy is indiscriminate. Our bodies can turn against us despite our very best efforts.

But I know with complete certainty that an increasing number of people who were "old enough to die" are recovering from major setbacks and enjoying decades of passionate, purposeful, meaningful and significant life. They're able to recover because they were prehabilitated. They took advantage of modern medicine and were willing to put in the work. They didn't buy into the ageist belief that pursuing positive lifestyle modification is appropriate for a 20-year-old but not for a 75-year-old.

Dismissing the benefits of exercise because it doesn't *guarantee* longevity, or conflating the desire to exercise with the pursuit of immortality, is ridiculous.

Muscle Memory

One of the major benefits of prehabilitation is banking muscle memory. This is illustrated by the fact that many former athletes rapidly regain strength and muscle development when they return to their sport. You've experienced this same phenomenon if you've spent any amount of time lifting weights, then taken a break and later started lifting again. You get stronger more quickly than you did the first time. It turns out that muscle fibers actually do have a kind of "memory."

The simple explanation for this memory is that unlike other cells, muscle cells are multinucleated. They contain not just one nucleus but many. Resistance training has been shown to increase the number of nuclei in muscle fibers, which, in turn, allows those fibers to grow larger.

If we don't use our muscles as we age, they'll lose size and strength. But recent research suggests that the additional nuclei created — even long ago, during periods of vigorous exercise — never go away. They lie dormant until exposed to vigorous exercise again, at which time they enable rapid redevelopment of muscle fiber.

This means that not only will the exercise that you engaged

in years ago help you regain strength and fitness today, any exercise that you do now will benefit you in the future — even if you were to stop doing it for years. In other words, you can literally bank future fitness.

This reason alone should be enough to inspire us to immediately begin prehabilitating with some form of resistance training or vigorous exercise in preparation for the inevitable health challenges of aging.

Orville Rogers: Never Giving Up

Orville Rogers started running at age 50. In 1993, at age 75, he underwent multiple bypass surgery to correct six blocked arteries. His overall conditioning at the time of his surgery — he had been prehabilitated — enabled him to recover quickly and resume running.

At age 90, Orville entered his first competitive track meet, quickly setting two world age-group records. In 2011, at age 93, he suffered a stroke that left him totally paralyzed in his left foot and left hand, and partially paralyzed in his left hip.

Most 93-year-olds would never fully recover from a setback of that magnitude. Not only would their minds not allow it, their family, friends, caregivers and even doctors — under the influence of the Machine — wouldn't actively support it. "You've lived a good life," they'd say. "Relax and take it easy. Save your strength."

Orville immediately rejected the notion of "taking it easy." To him, it wasn't an option. He wanted to return to the active, adventurous life that he loved, and demanded that his doctor devise the most rigorous rehab program possible. Orville spent nearly two weeks living in a rehabilitation hospital followed by several months as a daily outpatient.

His stroke didn't sentence Orville to life in a wheelchair at a nursing home surrounded by frail elderly residents. His years of prehabilitation and his determination to achieve extreme recovery quickly put him back on track. He reengaged with the lifestyle and the people that he cherished, traveling to track meets and setting nearly a dozen new world records. "You can never give up," he said. "You have to fight to achieve and then retain the ability to do the things that you love."

Don't dismiss Orville's example as unrealistic. He wasn't a lifelong athlete to whom active longevity came easily. It didn't come to him at all. He had to go and get it. His overall conditioning at the time of his two major health challenges gave him the opportunity to battle back. But it was his determination, dedication and ability to endure difficult and painful rehabilitation that turned his opportunity into reality. His refusal to let the Machine convince him he was too old to harness the strength required to recover from major health setbacks in his 90s allowed him to resume the life that he loved.

Roselio Muniz: Top of the Mountain

Growing Bolder interviewed 101-year-old Roselio Muniz in his home, where he shared his excitement about an upcoming vacation. Roselio was preparing to travel 4,750 miles for a return trip to Hawaii, where he had climbed a volcanic mountain at age 92. What made his story all the more remarkable was that he had undergone a complete knee replacement procedure just three months before that climb.

The first doctor Roselio visited refused to do the surgery. "He said, 'No, you can't have it. At your age, it's impossible,'" Roselio recalled. So, he sought a second opinion and found a doctor willing to look past the number on his birth certificate.

Dr. Hugh Morris was impressed with Roselio's attitude and his overall fitness level. "He was extremely healthy for 92, but his arthritis had become so severe that he could no longer walk without great pain and effort," Dr. Morris said. "He was highly motivated to continue his active lifestyle. And after a thorough evaluation, we determined that he was an excellent candidate for a knee replacement and I performed the procedure."

Three months later, Roselio was in Hawaii and sent a picture of himself climbing the mountain to Dr. Morris. "He couldn't believe it," Roselio said. "He was amazed." Roselio's brisk morning walks and his daily two-hour workouts on his stationary bicycle had prehabilitated him for the surgery, and all but guaranteed a quick recovery.

It was prehabilitation that got Roselio his new knee. It was prehabilitation that got Roselio to the top of the mountain, and it was prehabilitation that would enable his second vacation to those islands at age 101.

Susan Helmrich: Saved by Exercise

Susan Helmrich's entire adult life has been impacted by one of the biggest drug disasters in U.S. history — an unconscionable deception in which the bottom line trumped the common good.

Susan is now in her 60s, and even she's surprised that she's still alive. "I'm missing my entire reproductive system, one lung, my gall bladder, my duodenum, half of my pancreas and everything from my liver has been rerouted," she said. "You can't imagine that your body can function without all of these body parts. But here I am. It's kind of astonishing."

We interviewed Susan seconds before she climbed onto the starting blocks at the U.S. Masters Swimming National Championships. A world-ranked swimmer in multiple events, Susan has battled and beaten three very serious cancers thanks to her never-ending prehabilitation in a swimming pool.

Her nightmare began in the late 1970s, after she graduated from Syracuse University and was diagnosed with a rare vaginal cancer — a hallmark of DES (Diethylstilbestrol) exposure in the womb. DES, the first synthetic form of estrogen, was thought to prevent miscarriages. It was approved by the FDA without controlled studies, and beginning in the late 1940s was prescribed to 10 million women worldwide, including Susan's mother.

By the mid-1950s, research clearly revealed that DES not only didn't work, it was potentially toxic and carcinogenic. But it was a big moneymaker for more than 275 U.S. drug companies. It wasn't until 1971, nearly two decades after it was deemed dangerous, that it was finally removed from the market.

But it was too little, too late for 2 million DES daughters who were already beginning to experience the drug's devastating legacy. In a nearly 11-hour operation, Susan's life and her body were changed forever. "They removed basically everything: my vagina, my uterus, lymph nodes. They reconstructed my vagina with my colon, which required two more operations and 10 hospital stays over the next three years. I was 21 years old."

During this time, she found hope and strength in a swimming pool. "Without swimming I don't think I would have survived," she said. "I really don't."

Cancer-free for two decades, Susan was diagnosed with lung cancer in 1999 —even though she had never smoked a single cigarette. Doctors removed nearly her entire left lung. And once again, she got right back into the pool in an effort to recapture her life.

A decade later, in 2009, Susan was diagnosed with a rare form of pancreatic cancer. Doctors removed half of her pancreas and parts of her bowel and stomach, as well as her gall bladder, her bile duct and many of her remaining lymph nodes while rewiring her digestive tract. Weeks after her surgery, Susan was back in the pool — and it didn't go well. "I swam two laps and burst into tears," she said. "I was so weak and in such intense pain that I thought I'd never swim again. My husband reminded me that it was worse when I had my lung removed, so I kept going. Swimming has taught me that if you keep at it, you get slightly better every day."

Susan has overcome the impact of one of the darkest chapters in U.S. pharmaceutical history. She's done it because she never stops prehabilitating for her next challenge. "You can't stop moving," she said. "It was swimming for me, but almost any type of vigorous exercise will do. Exercise has saved my life, literally three times."

We're all mortal beings, and we'll all suffer physical setbacks as we age. It comes with the territory. Prehabilitating for these setbacks can mean the difference between grim decline and extreme recovery. Prehabilitation is one of the most important keys to active longevity. It can save hundreds of thousands, if not millions, of dollars in healthcare costs during your final decades. It's the key to solving the longevity paradox.

CHAPTER 13

THE HEALTH-WEALTH CONNECTION

——

Solving the Longevity Paradox

> 66
> —
> *In spite of illness, in spite even of the archenemy sorrow, one can remain alive long past the usual date of disintegration if one is unafraid of change, insatiable in intellectual curiosity, interested in big things, and happy in small ways.*
> —EDITH WHARTON

A MAJOR CRISIS IS UNFOLDING at the intersection of major medical and technological advances, rising healthcare costs and a rapidly aging — and mostly unhealthy — population.

Actuaries are now calculating what they call "longevity risk," which is the very real and rising risk that many of us will outlive our money. That's the longevity paradox: *The thing that we most aspire to in the future (longevity) is the greatest threat to that future.*

Of course, part of the answer is to plan, save, invest and reduce spending. But the real solution to the longevity paradox is found in the health-wealth connection. The single most important investment that we can make today — and the one investment that will provide the greatest overall returns in the years and decades ahead — involves no money and is therefore affordable to everyone. It's PLM, or positive lifestyle modification.

PLM is the most powerful and cost-effective form of healthcare. It can make whatever retirement savings we now have, or might accumulate, last longer and go further by lowering our future healthcare costs.

Thanks to transformative and exponential advances in technology and medicine, we can increasingly expect to not die from cancer or heart disease, which will come to be regarded as long-term chronic illnesses. We may not cure them, but we'll be able to live with them. And hopefully in the not too distant future, there'll be therapies to prevent neurodegenerative diseases such as Alzheimer's and Parkinson's.

Don't be deceived by the implications of these advances. Healthcare costs will continue to rise, and chronic illness will continue to be the single biggest driver of those costs. More than 60 percent of people over age 65 — and more than 70 percent of people over age 80 — live with one or more chronic diseases. The result for many families is financial ruin. Yet we continue to live as if we're indestructible and have limitless resources to buy our way out of future health crises.

A major healthcare group asked me to speak to their senior leadership about the challenges of meeting the healthcare needs of seniors. Like all healthcare providers, this hospital chain is struggling to deal with the rapidly increasing number of frail elderly people with critical healthcare needs but little to no money to pay for them. They invited me because they knew what I'd say: Healthcare for seniors must be delivered decades earlier in the form of positive lifestyle modification.

We can't ignore the needs of the frail elderly. But we must face the reality that dramatically transforming the lifestyle of a bedridden 85-year-old suffering the effects of decades of chronic illness is unlikely to happen. If healthcare systems are overwhelmed with frail elderly people now, just wait 20 years when the age wave is delivering thousands more every single day: men and women who are depressed, deconditioned, disabled, afflicted with dementia and suffering from an array of diseases and chronic illnesses.

The most effective and perhaps the only solution to this growing crisis is to change the lifestyle habits of younger adults. Will this prevent them from ever becoming frail elderly? Not likely, but it will dramatically compress the amount of time that they're frail. It will improve their response to treatment, reduce the length and frequency of their hospital visits and speed their recovery from illnesses. All of which will dramatically reduce the financial burden of their healthcare on their families, insurance companies and society in general.

For decades, we've had a late stage "pills and procedures"

approach to healthcare delivery. It's been a reactive model of care. Fortunately, the best providers are pivoting, as quickly as possible, from *sick care* to *well care*. They're becoming proactive, focusing more resources on prevention and wellbeing. They're providing positive lifestyle support and services, including nutrition counseling, wellness expos and medically certified fitness regimens, in addition to weight loss and smoking cessation programs. These efforts are producing better outcomes, reducing the cost of care for complex conditions and saving millions of lives and trillions of dollars in potential future costs.

The challenge, as always, is to get adults to actively participate in these programs — to get them to start Growing Bolder. Once again, it's a culture challenge. It's a belief system challenge. Baby boomers are the most diverse demographic group in history, and while there are many who pursue healthy lifestyles, the majority don't. Compared to previous generations, boomers have a higher incidence of chronic disease and are less likely to be engaged in regular exercise.

The average baby boomer has about $164,000 saved for retirement, according to the Economic Policy Institute. This is the average savings. The *median* savings for baby boomers nearing retirement is just $17,000, and a frightening 41 percent have no retirement savings at all. That's the bad news.

The worse news is that Social Security pays the average recipient $1,360 a month, which equates to $16,320 yearly. The average healthy couple will need nearly $400,000 for healthcare in their retirement years, and Medicare may only pay 51 percent of those costs. That's for a healthy couple, and it doesn't include long-term care, which 7 in 10 people are likely to need. Long-term care costs an additional $50,000 to $100,000 per year. And it isn't covered by Medicare.

Medicaid is the safety net program for people who have no means of paying for care. Medicaid does cover long-term care costs, but with few exceptions you will be required to spend down all of your assets before qualifying for Medicaid. Medicaid does not provide around-the-clock home care or allow you to choose your assisted living facility. In fact, you or your family will have little say over any of your care options once you are on Medicaid.

This is a fact not lost on boomers. Several surveys indicate that their number one fear — greater even than dementia, cancer or death itself — is running out of money before running out of time. And yet, many still lack the motivation to engage in positive lifestyle modification.

The importance of leveraging the health-wealth connection is especially true for women, who suffer the effects of ageism far more disproportionately than do men.

If a woman is in good health by age 30, she can still expect to pay $118,632 more on average over her lifetime for healthcare than a man. In addition, she'll likely make 77 cents for every dollar a man makes, thereby losing $500,000 over her lifetime due to the gender wage gap. And that's just the tip of the financial challenge iceberg faced by women as they age because women:

- Live four years longer but, on average, work twelve years fewer than men, thereby contributing less to their retirement plans.
- Are more likely to work part-time jobs that don't offer retirement plans.
- Are more likely to interrupt their careers to become caregivers.

- Are three times more likely to live alone when they reach old age.
- On average, live 14 years after the death of their husbands.

There are also disproportionate financial challenges faced by women who divorce later in life — a rapidly growing trend. While America's overall divorce rates are leveling off, divorce among baby boomers doubled between 1990 and 2010 — and many women are financially unprepared. Many deferred their educations or gave up jobs to raise children, and took breaks to care for aging parents. All of that can diminish their marketable job skills and hamper their ability to rejoin the labor market — especially in our ageist culture.

The result is that 22 percent of divorced women over age 80 are now living in poverty, compared to 15 percent of widowed women and 17 percent of women who never married, according to the National Center for Family & Marriage Research and the Social Security Administration.

Jean Chatzky, NBC financial editor and author of nearly a dozen books including her latest, "Age Proof: Living Longer Without Running Out of Money or Breaking a Hip," recommends amassing a retirement fund that totals at least 10 times your annual salary. "People are living longer, and the longer you live the longer you're going to live," she said. "You need enough money to go the distance."

Planning is the key to successfully navigating the financial needs of retirement, and that process can't begin too soon. I'll leave it to your financial planner to make recommendations on how best to manage your money. But always remember the health-wealth connection. Positive lifestyle modification is the most effective and least expensive healthcare plan. That should make it the foundation of any financial plan.

Understanding the health-wealth connection is one of the most important concepts to take away from this book. We are adding a new generation to our lives and we can't finance a 40-year retirement with a 30-year career. We can't improve our overall health and wellbeing without also improving our overall financial health. The two are inextricably linked. All the money in the world can't buy good health. But good health can save hundreds of thousands of dollars over our lifetimes.

CHAPTER 14

A LAUNCH PAD TO WHAT'S NEXT

—

Don't Retire—Aspire

66 *Twenty years from now you will be more
disappointed by the things that you didn't
do than by the ones you did do. So throw
off the bowlines. Sail away from the safe
harbor. Catch the trade winds in your sails.
Explore. Dream. Discover.*
—H. JACKSON BROWN, JR.

RETIREMENT IS DEFINED AS withdrawing and receding, the removal of something from service or use. It's a none-too-subtle way of saying that the workplace — and by extension, our culture — believes that we've reached a point of diminishing returns. Put another way, it's assumed that our skills, stamina, creativity and ability have depreciated to the point that we're no longer able to contribute in a way that justifies our salaries or continued investments in our futures.

Congratulations! Here's a gold watch to mark time as you busy yourself with bingo and crossword puzzles.

Don't blame baby boomers for not wanting to retire at 65. Thank them. They're crushing outdated social norms and reimagining, redefining and redesigning a life stage that will offer new options to enhance the lives of everyone who follows.

The mere notion that 65 is the beginning of the end would be laughable were it not so damaging. The U.S. passed the Social Security Act in 1935, specifying 65 as the age at which retirees could receive full benefits. Life expectancy at the time was 62. In other words, the average American died three years *before* becoming eligible to receive any benefits.

For generations, the difficulty in even reaching retirement age — and the relatively little time left for those who did — resulted in the entire concept becoming associated with a quick transition from relaxing, to withdrawing, to declining. Retirement was a sort of hospice — a chance to make yourself comfortable at home while getting your affairs in order and awaiting a rapidly approaching death.

The average age of someone moving into a nursing home was 65 back in the 1960s. Today it's 81. It's easy to see why we've established a damaging psychological and physiological connection between the age of 65, the concept of retirement and the ideology of decline. It's just as easy to see that we must destroy this connection before it destroys us. Of course, there must be an age at which the government begins providing Social Security benefits, but I'll leave that discussion for another time.

There's certainly nothing wrong with — and much that is beneficial about — ending a career, slowing down, relaxing, reflecting and re-prioritizing. But doing so shouldn't lead to the end of a productive, engaging and meaningful life. Retirement isn't the beginning of the end. It's the beginning of what's next. And, once again, you get to choose what's next. You don't have to aspire to a second career, climbing a mountain, starting a business or making a difference in the lives of others. It's only important to know that all are possible. There are many who simply want to transition from "doing" to "being." But the question becomes, being what?

Our lives are becoming increasingly non-linear with respect to major life events. There's no arbitrary age at which you automatically transition from one life stage to another, no pre-determined series of milestones attached to a calendar. You can go to school, change careers, start new businesses or pursue new relationships at any age.

You can start or work for a nonprofit, run for office or campaign for candidates who support your positions. You can join the Peace Corps, start a blog or build a website. Did you know that the fastest-growing group of first-time entrepreneurs is now women over the age of 50? Almost anything is possible, which is why we need coaches, guidance counselors, role models, business incubators and educational opportunities — all geared toward men and women in their 50s, 60s and 70s.

Most importantly, we need a new belief system. Because when imagining "what's next" we're limited by the accepted boundaries of possibility — and those boundaries have been drawn by the Machine.

The key to making the most of this new life stage is to overcome fear with action. Begin to view "retirement" as a pit stop. It's an opportunity to pull over for a moment and prepare for the next stage of the race: to refuel, change tires and discuss strategies. Remember, every pit stop ends the same way: by stepping on the gas and pulling back onto the racetrack — not by shutting down the engine.

Now is the time to look at life through a new lens that isn't distorted by obligation. The things that defined us for decades are gone. If you're retired, your job no longer defines you. If you're an empty nester, your children no longer define you. If you're widowed or divorced, your spouse no longer defines you. When the shackles of expectation are removed, there is an emancipation that comes with growing older.

Discovering your true and authentic self is liberating. But it's also difficult and frightening, at least at first. The poet e.e. cummings said: "To be nobody-but-yourself — in a world which is doing its best, night and day, to make you everybody else — means to fight the hardest battle which any human being can fight."

And it gets harder as we grow older, because we've been told for so long what's *not* possible that few of us know what *is* possible. If life is a play, there are countless roles for young people but very few for older people. We can't be afraid to write our own scripts and cast ourselves in whatever roles we want. Now is the time for personal liberation.

While finances are important, we should now prioritize

meaning over money. We should always be moving toward more satisfaction and more significance. Most of us, of course, will need to find a way to get paid. But we should get paid for doing things that we'd do anyway; for doing things that make us want to spring out of bed every morning. Even those who've saved enough to live comfortably to 100 without working another day should aggressively pursue personal growth. We don't grow old. When we stop growing, we become old.

If you're in your 20s or 30 or 40s, find a way to do something you love that gives meaning to your life. Even if you can't make a living at it, do it part-time or as a volunteer or intern. Actively cultivate and nurture connections inside your passions. The greatest gift you can give your future self is the ability to make a living beyond age 65 at something that you enjoy. Passion is what keeps us alive — and being able to monetize our passions as we age is the gift that keeps on giving.

Roger McGuinn, founder of the Byrds and a Rock and Roll Hall of Famer, is a Growing Bolder contributor. He's been featured in the opening of the Growing Bolder TV show, during which he implores viewers to "find something you love and make it your lifestyle." Roger said: "I'm inspired by [classical guitarist] Andrés Segovia. He was booked at Carnegie Hall when he was 93. The only reason he didn't show up is that he died. That's how I want to live my life."

Comedian George Burns was booked to play both the Palladium in London and Caesars Palace in Las Vegas for his 100th birthday. "How can I die? I'm booked!" was one of his go-to jokes. It was a funny line, but it contained a powerful truth. The week he turned 100, Burns wasn't well and had to cancel both shows. He died just a couple of months later. But those who knew him best said that continuing to book dates is what kept him active, engaged and enjoying life all the way to the century mark.

Research into mortality rates reveals that the later we retire, the longer we live. Because without purpose and discipline, we're more prone to developing unhealthy habits such as drinking too much, eating poorly and not making time for socialization. We're also more likely to become physically inactive. Unfortunately, many live on an ageist autopilot and can't wait to stop working and withdraw. They hate their work, are in poor overall health, have little energy and are uninterested in reinventing themselves. In most cases, they're not financially prepared to stop working, don't have long-term health insurance and are making daily lifestyle choices that will invariably lead to chronic illness, dwindling finances, increased isolation and a gradual loss of independence.

I'll admit to being more than a little jealous of those who knew from a very early age what their "true purpose" in life was and have been happily pursuing it ever since. They engage daily in activities from which they never retire because they consider what they do to be more of a calling than a career. For most of us, it hasn't been that easy. We followed an education and career path based on the dreams of our parents, the results of an 8th-grade aptitude test or the suggestions of a high school guidance counselor who was really an assistant football coach needing something to do before practice.

The good news is that it's almost never too late to discover our true selves and reinvent our daily lives. I say "almost" never too late because, once again, we can't ignore the reality that our days are numbered. Optimistically, that number is 32,850 days, if we live to age 90. By the time we're 65, there are only 9,125 days left. The real question is, how many of those days will we enjoy? How many will be spent enjoying good health, clear thinking and a profound sense of passion and purpose? How many will be spent doing something other than marking time and waiting for the end?

More than 80 percent of Americans are unhappy with our jobs, careers or family lives. That's a tragic failure because human beings are wired for success and pleasure and our overall happiness should increase as we age. When a shortening time horizon becomes an unavoidable reality, suddenly we are encouraged, if not forced, to live in the moment. Older adults have accepted or at least become more comfortable with the past and grown less worried about the future. This ability to dwell in the present and expand the now is largely responsible for the U-Curve of happiness demonstrated in the results of multiple surveys and studies. These studies found that as young adults we are generally happy, before happiness wanes in our 30s and 40s when we're faced with the challenges of adulthood. In our 50s and 60s we begin to grow happier until human happiness peaks in our 70s and 80s. Given the number of nonagenarians who have told us that their 90s became the best decade of their life, I think it's safe to assume that future research will indicate that human happiness has the potential to peak in our 90s.

Of course, this is only the *potential* for happiness. Many older people are miserable. Perhaps this "happiness disconnect" is because we've spent years making safe career and personal choices and now find change too risky. Our lives stagnate and we enter a period of pathological stasis, a life-limiting, soul-killing withdrawal from the flow of life.

Now, though, is the time to take risks. Fear of failure is gone — or should be. There's no longer any pressure to please our parents or teachers. If necessity is the mother of invention, opportunity is the mother of reinvention. Seize the opportunity of this new life stage to discover the passion that lies within.

Remember that we're not made to withdraw from life; we're made to lean into it. We're made to confront the lion and outthink the fox. We're made to be bold, to take risks and explore new territory. We're made to help others and to protect the weak and infirm in our tribes. We're the greatest problem-solving, ass-kicking, fearless, selfless, empathetic animals that have ever walked the face of the earth. We didn't choose to be all that; it chose us. It's in our DNA. Let's quit suppressing it and start expressing it. We're nothing short of magnificent. We should own it.

But finding our way forward isn't always easy, even for "America's Sweetheart."

Jane Pauley: The Reinvention Evangelist

"I kind of waited for the phone to ring. It always had. It didn't this time," Jane Pauley said. "I knew I wasn't retired. I was just 54 and expected to do more. But I didn't know what."

It was a turning point for Pauley, the broadcasting legend who always seemed to stumble into opportunity. Jobs and assignments often were served up on a silver platter at NBC anchor Tom Brokaw's dinner parties. Even her husband of nearly four decades, renowned Doonesbury cartoonist Garry Trudeau, was introduced to her at a dinner hosted by Brokaw.

But now, for the first time since she was hired by WISH-TV in Indianapolis at the age of 21, Pauley was in unfamiliar territory. Suddenly and surprisingly, in her mid-50s, life stopped "just happening" for the woman once dubbed by the media "America's Sweetheart."

"I'm a little embarrassed to admit this, but it took four years of poking around to find something new," Pauley recalled. "And I wasn't just sitting on my sofa watching the Home Shopping Network. I was really working the problem. It took getting up and doing something, which inspired something else. I made it happen."

Pauley is proud of her eventual accomplishment, primarily because she's not the Type-A, obsessively driven personality that typically gravitates to the pace and power of network news. For most of her life, options were created for her or offered to her. Her role was basically choosing which ones to accept.

From 1976 to 1989, Pauley was co-host, first with Brokaw and later with Bryant Gumbel, of NBC's Today. After leaving Today amid very public speculation that she was being forced out in favor of the younger Deborah Norville, Pauley hosted *Real Life with Jane Pauley*, a newsmagazine show with an upbeat focus. The show lasted only one season, but NBC continued finding high-profile projects for her.

She joined another newsmagazine, *Dateline NBC*, as co-host with Stone Phillips. She remained there until 2003, then hosted a syndicated daytime talk show that was cancelled after only eight months. That's when the phone stopped ringing and Pauley began to think that her days in broadcasting might be over.

In 2005, Pauley revealed her personal battle with bipolar disorder in her bestselling memoir, "Skywriting: A Life Out of the Blue." The book helped destigmatize depression but did little to reignite her stalled broadcasting career. She realized, for the first time, that simply waiting for opportunity to come her way was no longer an option. She had to make something happen.

"Part of my message these days is the importance of making something happen," she said. And that's what she did. She talked her way back onto Today as a contributor to "Your Life Calling," a monthly series in which she shared the stories of men and women creating new opportunities in middle age.

She used her new platform to write a second bestseller, "Your Life Calling: Reimagining the Rest of Your Life." The former news anchor had become a reinvention evangelist. "Frankly I'm not a person who lives the message I espouse," she admitted. "I'm not an adventure seeker. I'm not the most curious person you know. I'm really comfortable right here on this sofa. When it comes to the importance of creating change and making things happen, I need to hear myself say it in order to live it."

When "Your Life Calling" was cancelled after four years, Pauley's phone *did* ring, and she was offered what she calls her "dream job" as a correspondent for CBS Sunday Morning with Charles Osgood. She worked as a contributor and substitute host for nearly two years until, at age 65, she became only the third host in the show's history, succeeding Osgood when he retired at age 83 after 22 years on the show.

Pauley wouldn't mind if her job with CBS Sunday Morning was her last. But if it's not, she no longer fears the future now that she's learned the importance of taking action and the power of a single first step. "That first step can introduce you to incredibly rewarding opportunities," she said. "But unless you take that first step, nothing will happen. Inspiration and opportunity are everywhere, but you have to be looking."

Pauley has learned to embrace her age, even in an industry known for being ageist. "Getting older is not the same as getting old," she insisted. "Middle age can now last into our

70s or 80s. We have to recalibrate how we define middle age and how we act. We have to keep moving forward."

Even Jane Pauley learned that the phone stops ringing. If she felt lost and no longer needed, it's easy to understand the fear and frustration that most of us experience when wondering what's next — or if there'll even *be* a next.

Many employers are actively pushing older workers out the door. And few are willing to hire older employees because they've been branded by the ageist propaganda machine as undesirable, with rapidly diminishing skills and rapidly increasing needs. We should all stand up against ageism and demand equal employment opportunities. But change is slow, and many of us don't have time to wait for society to treat us fairly. We must take control of our own lives and create our own opportunities.

If we're going to turn the concept of retirement into a launch pad to what's next, we must learn to embrace risk and discover the magic of saying "yes!"

CHAPTER 15

RETHINKING RISK

*The Life-Expanding Power
of Saying Yes!*

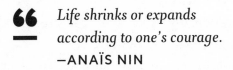 *Life shrinks or expands
according to one's courage.*
—ANAÏS NIN

ONE OF THE MOST DIFFICULT AND IMPORTANT challenges we face as we age is balancing the need for safety with the basic human need for experience. In 2012, Dr. Bill Thomas, the man who started the movement to deinstitutionalize the nursing-care industry, began talking about the concept of "surplus safety," which he defined as an unhealthy obsession with avoiding downside risk (what might go wrong) while eliminating the possibility of upside risk (better-than-expected outcomes).

Though Dr. Thomas was talking about life in nursing homes, I believe the concept of surplus safety has crept into all our of lives. The ageist propaganda machine has convinced us that there's very little upside to risk-taking as we age, so why take any risks in the first place?

It has convinced us that we've reached or are approaching a point of diminishing ability, and that our strategy moving forward should be to not extend ourselves in any way. It's time to pull our heads inside our shells and hunker down.

There's no denying that safety is critically important. But equally important is quality of life. Human beings, by nature, need autonomy, love, novelty and thrive on experience. Without some degree of each, it's fair to question if life is even worth living.

Growing Bolder is about the need to confront life and chase experiences, not retreat and withdraw. The more we're exposed to the possibilities of aging, the more we begin to understand the value of risk-taking and the dangers of surplus safety. Risk-taking, especially as we age, leads to the kind of experiences that make life worth living.

I'm not talking about unnecessary physical risks. Participating in activities in which the prospect for serious injury is great, when you're not prepared for those activities, is stupid. But to take away all risks and all opportunities to make mistakes is to take away what it means to be human. We must learn to balance risk tolerance, so we don't simply wither away, strapped to a bed. When we allow surplus safety to creep into our lives and control our behavior, we eliminate the opportunity for the kinds of experiences that make life worth living.

We interviewed Julia "Hurricane" Hawkins the week after she broke the world record in the 100-meter dash in the 100-104 age group at the U.S. Masters National Championships. Julia didn't begin running until she was 100, and this was just her second competition ever.

I reminded Julia that most people gradually become totally risk-averse as they age, and may eventually choose to stay in their homes, their chairs or even their beds where they feel safest. "Weren't you afraid?" I asked. She admitted: "I was scared to death. I was afraid I'd fall and break my hip. I was afraid I'd embarrass my family. I was afraid that I might have a heart attack or a stroke. I was afraid I might die on the track. I was so afraid that I even took care of a few things at home just in case I never came back. Yes, I was afraid. But I looked that fear in the face and I ran. That's what you must do as you grow older. You must continually face your fears."

Boom! Julie dropped a major truth bomb. The key to Growing Bolder is that idea: "I looked that fear in the face and I ran." We're confronted with countless fears throughout our lives, and we either move forward in the face of those fears or we back down. Those who maintain a high quality of life into their 90s and even 100s aren't the backing-down types. They either live independently and can make their own decisions, or they're surrounded by others who allow them the dignity of choice and help them pursue their passions while mitigating risk.

Julia told us that she wanted to inspire her family, and she wanted the life experience. Not only did she not fall, embarrass herself or die, she became an international celebrity overnight. Video of her remarkable run went viral on social media, and reports of her accomplishment were featured on newscasts across the globe. "I'm so honored and humbled by all of the attention," she said. "Mostly, I'm happy that I can inspire other older people to get moving. The risk was worth the reward."

We've all heard the axiom: "You can't teach an old dog new tricks." It's been around for centuries. Its meaning has nothing to do with dogs and tricks and everything to do with people and learning. The truth is that we're never too old to learn. And yet we readily dismiss the possibility because of some silly sentiment written nearly 500 years ago and perpetuated to this day by the Machine.

The real issue is not our inability to continue learning. In many ways, our capacity to learn increases as we age. The real issue is our unwillingness to continue taking risks. When people realize that their lives are almost over, they mourn for passions not pursued and risks not taken. Dr. Thomas is very straightforward in his prescription for successful aging: "Take risks!"

The first step in taking risk and seizing the opportunity of aging is learning to say yes. The Machine constantly reinforces a *culture of no* as we age. It convinces us that it's natural for our world to shrink, and that "no" is the appropriate, safe and sensible answer to nearly every opportunity that involves getting off the couch.

Saying no is the kiss of death, while saying yes is the breath of life. It's really that simple. Say no enough times and your life will very quickly be reduced to an easy chair, a dinner tray, a TV and a bed. Saying yes leads to an ever-expanding social circle, opportunity, adventure, passion and purpose — all of which are critical to active longevity.

Saying no is the growing older response to advancing years. Saying yes is the Growing Bolder response.

Saying yes is the mantra of my friend and colleague Wendy Chioji. Wendy walked away from a 25-year career as a popular and successful TV news anchor after fighting a very public battle with breast cancer. "It redefines how you look at things because, suddenly, it's like maybe you have next year and maybe you don't," Wendy said. "So, you have to go for it right now."

Wendy's life-threatening diagnosis led to a life-changing epiphany. "It was definitely a Growing Bolder moment for me," she remembered. "I realized that we really only have one shot at this. Everything we do has to make a difference. Everything we do has to matter. I committed to living big and bold, taking calculated risks and doing whatever I can to help others. Once you face your mortality, there's no longer a fear of failure."

Wendy quit her job, sold her house and moved to Utah, where she became a full-time badass in the best sense of the word: blogger, traveler, world-class triathlete, adventure racer, ski bum, part-time correspondent for the Sundance Film Festival and host of Growing Bolder's Surviving & Thriving television program.

Unfortunately, Wendy's battle with cancer wasn't over. She's now battling a rare form of incurable cancer called recurrent thymic carcinoma. After participating in three clinical trials Wendy is enrolled in a fourth as she continues looking for "what's next" in her never-ending effort to "buy time" until her cancer can be controlled, if not cured.

Wendy has refused to let cancer steal her passion for life.

In fact, it has given her a passion beyond any she experienced pre-diagnosis. It has rearranged her priorities, forced her to live in the moment and resulted in the personal mantra by which she now lives: "Say yes!"

Surviving a serious health battle is a major disruptor to the Machine. It clears the fog and reveals the stark but empowering truth that we're mortal beings, and as such we're facing a terminal diagnosis — and the clock is ticking. Why does it take a deadly disease to help us realize that every minute is priceless and filled with endless opportunity?

But opportunity doesn't happen to us, we happen to it. And it all begins with a single word: Yes.

Conquering Kilimanjaro

A few years ago, I learned that Wendy and another good friend, Dr. Robert Masson, a renowned spine surgeon and the Growing Bolder medical director, were joining a team of cancer survivors and cancer community advocates in an attempt to summit Africa's Mount Kilimanjaro, the world's tallest free-standing mountain. While I thought it was a very cool idea, I never for an instant thought about going until Robert suggested it out of the blue. "You should come along," he encouraged, "and bring a video camera."

The trip was just a few months away. I was totally unprepared and didn't have the time or the money to spare. There were countless reasons to say no, and that's exactly what I said. But I kept hearing Wendy's voice in my head, whispering "say yes." And that's exactly what I did.

A short time later 16 men and women, most of whom had never met one another, arrived at the Kia Lodge in Arusha, Tanzania. I was the oldest and least prepared member of the group. I immediately began wondering what I was doing there. My doubts intensified when we learned that only 20 percent of all climbers reach Uhuru Peak, the highest of Kili's three summits at nearly 20,000 feet. In addition, I was told, about 100 people each year die from the attempt.

Mount Kilimanjaro is not a technical climb, but it's a grueling climb. Chris Warner, our expedition leader and one of the world's premiere high-altitude mountaineers, calls Kili "the most underestimated mountain in the world."

Despite that warning, within a few minutes of meeting one another the team came to a bold and spontaneous decision that made our odds of success even longer. We wanted to resist the standard practice of climbing in smaller, more efficient groups and commit to reaching the summit together — all 16 of us at the same time — or not at all.

If we were fortunate enough to make it to the summit, we could only remain for a short time before needing to descend. That meant that if we divided into smaller groups and reached the summit at different times, we wouldn't be able to pose together with our huge honor flag containing the names of loved ones and others whose lives were claimed by cancer. We wouldn't be able to send a message to the millions of survivors worldwide that life is worth fighting for.

Chris agreed to try and accommodate our request. But he told us that we'd have to learn to love one another very quickly or we'd fail. "Love is the only thing powerful enough to get all 16 of us to the summit together," he said. "Not your $500 sleeping bags, your $200 boots, your waterproof tents or your hot daily meals. Only love for one another will result in all 16 of us standing together on the summit, posing with our flag."

That seemed like a stretch to me. Most of us had never even

met one another. I wasn't yet sure if I even liked the others, so coming to love them seemed a bit far-fetched. Sure, the importance of teamwork was obvious. But I doubted that we'd be together long enough for a bond that strong to form.

Six days of climbing and sleeping in extreme conditions had taken its toll by the time we reached high camp, our last stop before the final push to the summit. We were exhausted and struggling for breath, but we'd grown closer with every labored step up the mountain. Chris taught us that there was no such thing as an "individual load" or "individual resource." There was only "group load" and "group resource." We shared everything: coats, food, water, laughs, fears and encouragement. We paid close attention to one another, constantly asking: "Are you OK? Do you need anything? Can I carry that for you?"

At 11 p.m., in freezing temperatures and falling snow, we began what would be a nine-hour push to the summit. The environment turned increasingly hostile as we slogged through the darkness on steep, slippery and seemingly endless switchbacks. Headaches, nausea and doubt began to set in. Wendy was just six weeks removed from a difficult course of radiation therapy. "I started getting nose bleeds," she later confessed. "I could feel and taste the blood dripping down the back of my throat. My vision was starting to go. I started seeing really weird things. I was hypoxic. I couldn't talk, and for the first time I started to wonder if I could finish."

This was the most grueling — and yet the most magically surreal — stage of the entire expedition. There was a very real and palpable power pushing us forward, leading us upward. Chris had been right. The absolute reliance upon one another had forged a bond and created a force that wouldn't be stopped.

As the sun began to rise, we reached Gilman's Point, the

first of Kili's three summits. We pressed on to Stella Point, the second summit and another landmark at which many claim success and consider their journey finished. We paused only momentarily to enjoy the magnificence of the rising sun and to gather ourselves for the last excruciating, exhilarating stretch.

Seven days after taking our first step and nine hours after leaving high camp, all 16 of us reached the roof of Africa — Uhuru Peak — at 19,341 feet. We had conquered Kili together. By any standard, it was an incredible moment for everyone — but especially for the four cancer survivors: Wendy as well as Doug Ulman, Bree Sandlin and Jeremy Jungling. Among them, they'd battled the disease seven times. In many ways, this journey from the valley to the mountaintop was a metaphor for their shared experience.

While most climbers are able to remain on the summit for only a few minutes, we stayed for nearly an hour, enjoying the unique rush of shared accomplishment and honoring those for whom we had undertaken this adventure. Finally, fearing the growing effects of hypoxia and the potential for acute mountain sickness and cerebral or pulmonary edema, Chris ordered us to begin our long descent.

Two nights later, back at the lodge in Arusha while huddled around a fire pit, Chris told us: "An expedition is a success not because you reach the summit and live to tell about it. It's a success when you learn something about yourself that you can apply to life back home." He then challenged all of us to share what we had learned.

"It's a validation of just how tough we all are," Wendy offered. "You always think you've been pushed to your limit, that you can't handle any more. That's a lie. No matter what challenges we're facing, we can all keep moving forward. That knowledge is illuminating, uplifting, powerful, spiritual, emotional and impactful."

For Robert, the climb was a reaffirmation of what's truly important. "I return home with the realization that I don't want to focus so much on quantitative goals," he said. "I want to spend my time and energy in the pursuit of qualitative goals that feed my soul and enrich my life and the lives of others in meaningful ways."

For me, the major takeaway was what Chris had declared on day one: Only love can get us to the top of the mountain, whatever the mountain might be. I didn't get it at first, but now I'm a believer. To be successful in life, especially in our later years, we must surround ourselves with people who care about us and about whom we care. Love fuels the life force.

I took Robert's initial suggestion and made the climb with a video camera. It made what was already the most difficult challenge of my life even more difficult, but the result was worth the effort. Growing Bolder's Emmy-nominated documentary film "Conquering Kilimanjaro" has been used to raise money for the Livestrong Foundation and to provide hope and inspiration to anyone battling a serious health challenge.

It all happened because I was willing to take a risk and said the most important word in the Growing Bolder vocabulary: Yes!

CHAPTER 16

CONFRONTING THE CAREGIVING CRISIS

Creating a Culture of Care in an Ageist World

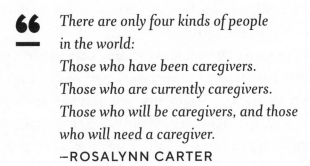

There are only four kinds of people in the world:
Those who have been caregivers.
Those who are currently caregivers.
Those who will be caregivers, and those who will need a caregiver.
—ROSALYNN CARTER

A NATIONAL CAREGIVING CRISIS is unfolding in an ageist society that enthusiastically demeans and diminishes the value of its elders. We're facing a demographic dilemma in the form of a growing care gap: a rapidly increasing number of older people requiring care, and fewer younger people able or willing to provide that care.

The aging of America, along with the desire to age in place and the rising cost of nursing care, has resulted in home care becoming the fastest-growing occupation in the country — and family caregivers becoming some of the most stressed and overworked members of our society.

The typical family caregiver is now a 46-year-old woman who has a job while also spending 18 hours a week caring for a parent who lives nearby. In addition, many are caring for children or grandchildren. To provide the best possible care, caregivers often sacrifice their own needs — and the emotional, physical and mental strain can be highly destructive.

The burden of caregiving can lead to extreme fatigue, poor eating, lack of exercise, increased use of medications and alcohol, loss of interest in work, decreased work production and withdrawal from friends. Studies reveal that caregivers' risk for experiencing depression is 30 times greater than that of non-caregivers with an alarming 91 percent of caregivers surveyed suffering from depression and acute stress. (National Institutes on Health, 2010 and Evercare Study of Caregivers in Decline, 2010).

This isn't a small problem. Providing care to adult relatives and friends has become a necessary part of everyday life for more than 45 million Americans — a number that's growing every year. These unpaid caregivers are the single most important component in addressing the growing challenge of senior healthcare. They provide nearly 50 billion hours of care each year, with an estimated value approaching $500 billion. Yet, not only are they unpaid, they typically spend more than $7,000 per year out of their own pockets on caregiving expenses.

Even professional caregivers are feeling the effects. More than 70 percent of nursing home staff need to be replaced each year due to caregiver burnout. Even for home care providers the turnover rate is as high as 60 percent.

It's hard to overstate the enormity of this growing crisis, which will test our culture in the decades ahead. Will we understand, value and support the enormous contributions of both unpaid and paid caregivers, or will we simply look the other way while this potentially overwhelming challenge destroys lives and families?

Will we provide the tools and training that home caregivers need to help those they care for find passion and purpose in their lives, no matter their age or condition? Will we provide the relief and respite necessary to help home caregivers maintain their own mental and physical health? Will we create and fund workplace policies to help family caregivers keep working? Will we provide the kind of financial support, including tax relief, that caregivers need and deserve?

The technical and clinical of aspects of caregiving are well-addressed. The real need is in life enrichment. The definition of "care" itself needs to be rewritten. Life is about living. It's not about being alive. How can we continue to push the boundaries of possibility when it comes to engaging in and creating moments of joy for those in our care? And, equally important, how can we help turn the caregiving journey into the life-enriching blessing for the caregiver that it has the potential to be, and not just the stress-filled, demoralizing experience that it becomes for millions of people?

If we did little more than learn to engage and support the elderly as we now do the disabled, we would be making monumental progress. We've created a world of technological and cultural accommodation for the disabled. We recognize the value of their lives and the need to provide pathways for inclusion. And yet when older people lose abilities and, in essence, become disabled, we shrug our shoulders and just try to keep them comfortable because "They're old, after all."

Caring for an aging parent is challenging and frustrating. But with preparation, planning and plenty of support it can also be a blessing and one of life's most meaningful experiences. We're robbing ourselves of this opportunity by not providing the support that caregivers need and deserve. It's a national tragedy.

Growing Bolder is trying to contribute through our "Art of Caregiving" series. We believe that a moment at age 85 or 95 is every bit as valuable as a moment at age 25 or 35. We know that even those in the advanced stages of dementia can experience love and joy. Our series is designed to help caregivers create those moments of joy and to remove some of the stress and pressure. Amy Cameron O'Rourke, a contributor to our series, says: "Don't put pressure on yourself to be a perfect caregiver. There's no such thing. I tell caregivers to lower their expectations. It's going to be messy, and that's OK." Caregiving can't be micromanaged because not only is every situation different, every day is different — and change is constant.

While we work to provide help to home caregivers, it's imperative that we also demand more out of the senior-living industry, including nursing homes, independent living and assisted-living facilities and continuing care retirement communities (CCRCs).

The industry spends a great deal of money providing activities meant to keep residents busy. But being busy is not the same as being engaged, and many of these programs are failing on both counts. Only 20 to 30 percent of all senior-living residents regularly participate in the activities offered. (Kay Van Norman, MS Creating Purpose Driven Communities, The Journal on Active Aging September/October 2009). What's responsible for this disconnect?

A Culture of Yes

I believe the senior-living industry is failing in two very important areas. First and foremost, it's failing to change the culture of aging within its communities. Many senior-living communities are bastions of ageism. Theirs is not an overt or odious form of ageism. These communities care about their residents. They want them to be happy and healthy. Yet they grossly underestimate the potential of older people. Therefore, they do little to promote the idea that more is possible. This attitude allows, if not encourages, withdrawal and decline — and it perpetuates institutionalized ageism.

Most older adults have been seriously impaired by the Machine and its ageist propaganda. They have a highly flawed sense of what they can and should be doing at their ages. They're frustrated, disappointed, pessimistic and afraid. Despite being surrounded by countless options for engagement, they've been programmed to withdraw. "No" has become the default answer when presented with new options and opportunities.

As we age, saying no leads to isolation and a rapidly shrinking world. Senior-living communities should identify daily opportunities for residents to say yes, while providing relatable examples of what happens when others like them say yes. They should celebrate those who *do* say yes and continue working with and encouraging those who don't say yes. A senior-living community might have the greatest programming ever, but that programming will fail every time inside a culture of no.

Creating a culture of yes becomes the foundation upon which active participation is built and quality of life is improved. How is this done? Once again, a good place to start is through the example of "someone like me." There are residents in every community who are hungry for experience and will demonstrate the power of yes if given the opportunity. Helping them to pursue their passions and sharing their examples with other residents will help persuade others to say yes, too.

Creating a culture of yes is critical to overcoming the obsessive fear of risk that has, for decades, led many nursing homes to strap residents to their beds or chairs so they can't move and risk injuring themselves.

Thankfully, the best companies are distancing themselves from the practice. But the concept of surplus safety persists on a wide scale. The industry must evolve from the all or nothing mindset that has been common for decades. All or nothing is easy. It's also destructive — and sentences the frail elderly to years of misery.

Encouraging and enabling each person to experience daily life, not just survive it, is an immense challenge. The only way to expand the boundaries of what's possible is to accept and manage reasonable risk inside a culture of yes.

Sue and the Horse

An activities director at one of the nation's top assisted-living companies shared with me the story of an 85-year-old client we'll call "Sue." Sue once owned a horse and asked if she might be able to ride a horse once again. The activity director's immediate thought was "absolutely not!" She imagined everything that might go wrong. The horse might bolt and throw Sue to the ground, breaking every bone in her body. Not only could Sue be injured or even killed, unhappy relatives would file major lawsuits. "It's not a risk worth taking," she thought. If Sue couldn't navigate her way around the nursing home without her walker, she certainly couldn't ride a horse.

The activity director was even more hesitant because Sue, like many 85-year-olds, also suffered from early-stage dementia. Did she even fully understand what she wanted? The easy answer was to refuse her request and keep her "safe."

But Sue persisted. "When can I ride a horse?" she asked daily. The activity director eventually contacted a local stable that offered programs for disabled children and wounded warriors. The owners were not only comfortable with the idea of a frail elderly woman riding a horse, they were very encouraging.

Several days before Sue's trip to the stable, the activity director shared the news with other residents, asking if they'd also like to ride a horse. They all declined with such indignation that the activity director was taken aback.

"She's going to fall and break her neck."

"How irresponsible!"

The comments came fast and furious from residents who, like most their age, were believers in the doctrine of despair espoused by the Machine.

But Sue wouldn't be dissuaded. Sensing that the others might learn something from the experience, the activity director invited them to tag along and watch. While no one wanted to ride, they all wanted to see the spectacle. Several vans filled with curious nursing home residents made their way across town to the stable.

A short brown mare named Missy was walked into a chute that had steps leading to a platform. There was also a hoist for those unable to manage the steps. Sue didn't hesitate. She refused the hoist and, with assistance on both sides, slowly climbed the steps. Once on the platform, she was gently lifted and strapped onto a special saddle with a high back. Missy was walked out of the barn, while Sue beamed from ear to ear. She held the reins tightly and stroked Missy's mane. What was scheduled to be a 30-minute, one-rider excursion stretched into two hours, because nearly every one of the nursing home residents — the very ones who had dismissed the idea as dangerous and silly — now wanted turns. The pictures of their rides are now displayed in their rooms and have been sent to their families. Sue's "outrageous and unsafe" request turned into a true life-enhancing excursion.

This story proves, once again, the power of an example from "someone like me," and the value of risk-taking inside a culture of yes.

Programming with Purpose

While creating a culture of yes is job one, senior-living communities should make reexamining their programming job two. Over the past 40 years, there has been very little change in programming for seniors, which is designed primarily to keep participants innocuously occupied. Sometimes I think the industry was modeled after childcare: "We'll keep your kid safe, and if we have time we'll try to actually connect with her and teach her something."

These days, the senior-living industry must be in the business of providing purpose. Senior-living communities must begin thinking of themselves as educational institutions with dynamic, responsive and continually evolving programming — no matter how old and frail their residents may be. I can hear the response now: "But that's not the business we're in!" To which I reply: "If you don't quickly *make* it your business, you won't be in business much longer."

There are certainly many things that the industry is doing well by today's standards. But those standards are rapidly changing. For years, if not decades, those aging into senior living have changed very little. Now they're changing overnight by leaps and bounds — and Growing Bolder is among those facilitating that change. We're working every day to change the mindset about what's possible, even for the frail elderly. Ultimately, the changing expectations of consumers will demand change from the senior-living industry — change that it has been slow to initiate on its own.

The senior living and caregiving industries should be leading, not resisting, this change. They should be incubators and accelerators for new ideas, constantly trying new ways to connect with and provide purpose for every resident. Their failure to do so has been shortsighted and ageist.

Many couples and individuals won't move into a senior-living community until they feel that they "have to" and that it's time to "give up." This mindset is because the industry has done little to convince them otherwise. Many CCRCs reinforce these perceptions with fear-based approaches to marketing: "We're close to the hospital!" "We have a defibrillator on every floor!" "Our hallways are large enough for walkers to go three-wide!" These are important features as one ages and should be noted. But when they become central to the primary marketing message, they serve mostly to reinforce negative stereotypes and the notion that moving into a senior-living community is, in fact, "giving up."

It's no wonder that many senior-living communities are struggling with low program participation rates. They're not only inheriting a negative and defeatist attitude among even their newest and youngest residents, they're also cultivating such an image.

There seems to be very little understanding that seniors are passionately purpose-driven. Creating a culture of yes and providing purpose-driven programming will resolve the problem of low participation rates overnight. Purpose-driven programs don't have to be sold to residents, because they appeal to basic human nature. They feed our never-ending need to contribute to our communities and to make a difference in the lives of others.

Seniors want to use their voices and leverage their skills and experience for beneficial purposes, but sadly are rarely given that opportunity. Successful senior programming provides opportunities to mentor young people, counsel businesspeople, feed the hungry, volunteer at schools, clean up the environment or comfort and rehabilitate injured animals.

I saw a story recently about a 99-year-old man who has been calling friends, neighbors, members of his church congregation and even strangers every day for 18 years and singing "Happy Birthday" to them. He estimated that he's made at least 35,000 calls. Without leaving his apartment, he has found a meaningful way to serve his community and says: "I wouldn't be alive without it."

I interviewed Gladys Naranjo, a Meals on Wheels client, as she anxiously awaited delivery of the daily meal that enabled her to remain in her small home. An 86-year-old widow, Gladys lives on a total income of $745 a month. It isn't just the daily visits and nutritional meals that keep Gladys alive — it's her passion for helping others. Gladys runs a 24/7 prayer line, taking calls at all hours and praying in Spanish or English for anyone needing help.

Providing true purpose to a group of residents is difficult enough. Providing purpose to individual residents is much harder, but should still be the goal of every senior-living community and every caregiver. What can happen when we begin to connect with each individual in a way that plugs into his or her passions and purposes?

Ruth 1898

One day we were sitting in the office wondering whatever became of Ruth Hamilton. Growing Bolder's Bill Shafer had produced several stories about Ruth while working for a local television station, including one at her 105th birthday celebration. Ruth reveled in the attention and amazed the party guests with her quick wit and contagious joy for living.

We checked the obituaries and found no indication that she'd passed away. So, we called the nursing home where Bill had last seen her. Amazingly she was still there, living on the top floor. We quickly arranged a visit and found Ruth asleep in a wheelchair. She was in a large room where a TV played loudly in one corner. There were many others like her, also in wheelchairs, wrapped in blankets and sound asleep.

Ruth was now 108 and, like most of the ultra elderly, she had outlived her spouse, her children and her friends. We were told that she hadn't received a single visitor in several years and had little to no engagement with the other residents.

We approached Ruth and lightly squeezed her arm. She slowly opened her eyes and peered at us from a place that seemed very far away. "Ruth, it's Bill Shafer and Marc Middleton. Remember us from TV?" The more we talked, the more responsive she became. It was as though we were pulling her back from a deep trance.

Bill knew all about Ruth's remarkable history. So, he began a one-sided conversation, asking about her marriage to a professional baseball player and her passion for teaching. He also asked her about being one of the first women to have her own radio show and being the first woman ever elected to the New Hampshire state Legislature. Bill reminded her that she had once taught diction to Hollywood starlets, seen Hitler in pre-war Germany and traveled all over the world giving lectures until late in life.

As Bill talked and Ruth listened, we began to see a glint of recognition and remembrance. Finally, she smiled and said: "I'm a teacher. I love to teach." Ruth was awake and the wheels were slowly turning when we finally left, promising to return soon.

We kept our promise, returning several times over the next few weeks. We always found Ruth as we did on that first visit — asleep in her wheelchair or in her bed. But on each successive visit, she would wake up and remember us more quickly. She was always eager to continue discussing and reconnecting with her past. By the end of each visit, she wasn't just talking, she was teaching — sharing with us the lessons learned from a lifetime of experience.

I took my laptop on one of our visits and pointed at the little dot above the screen, which I'm certain Ruth couldn't see. "This is a camera," I told her. "And I'm going to turn it on and you can talk about whatever you want. The camera will record a video of you, and we'll put that video on the internet where people all over the world can see it and learn from you."

We had introduced Ruth to the concept of video blogging — and the thought of having a global classroom totally energized her. "You mean my relatives in Denmark will see me?" she asked. "Everyone will see you," I answered. Ruth sat there in stunned silence for a moment. You could see the wheels turning. Finally she exclaimed, "How wonderful!"

We dubbed her RUTH 1898 (the year of her birth). And at age 108, she became the world's oldest blogger. Over the next 10 months, Ruth recorded dozens of videos, discussing such topics as the importance of curiosity, the power of prayer and the presidential election cycle. As promised, we shared her videos on GrowingBolder.com, where people all over the world were, in fact, inspired by her example.

Each time we visited to record a new video blog, we read Ruth the comments that had been generated by her previous one. She laughed in amazement and beamed with pride. This former teacher, who had outlived all her family and friends, was suddenly able to connect with people on the other side of the world from a wheelchair in a nursing home. That new reach — that new connection with humanity, that new opportunity to make a difference — gave Ruth purpose and passion. She felt useful and important again.

While there were activities at the nursing home where she lived, none were personal. They were simply group singalongs or TV time — which was really group nap time. For years, Ruth was wheeled out of her room every day for meals, during which she ate with a large group but was nonetheless alone. There was no real interaction or social connection. No one knew Ruth's story, nor did anyone make much effort to discover it and use it to engage her. There was no chance that any of the programs or activities offered would pull her out of her decline. She and those who cared for her were simply waiting for the inevitable. Her final days, months and years were on autopilot. Each day was a carbon copy of the one before until her journey was over.

We interrupted and disrupted. We changed the trajectory of Ruth's final days. We did it by simply knowing something about her past, understanding her passions and being willing to invest the time, effort and creativity to give her a purpose.

The first time we visited Ruth, she appeared almost comatose. The last few times, however, she was waiting for us camera-ready — in a dress with all her jewelry and a big smile on her face. Her transformation in appearance, but most especially in attitude and demeanor, was dramatic. I won't say we gave Ruth her life back. But we definitely gave her quality of life back after years of simply being alive.

Ruth died shortly before her 110th birthday. But she maintained a quick wit and her newly discovered joie de vivre until the very end. She represents what can happen, even for the ultra elderly, when someone is willing to try and connect in a way that's personally meaningful and provides purpose.

Success stories like Ruth's are waiting to be replicated in every kind of senior-living community. Creating an environment for those stories to unfold will not only result in profoundly important human benefits, but will also create an important differentiator — a competitive advantage — between communities.

Say No to the Chair

The overuse of wheelchairs is another growing problem in the caregiving industry today. Instilled with a fear of falling and a belief system that accelerates deconditioning, most older people are only too happy to sit down when wheelchair use is recommended. And it's recommended almost indiscriminately in a culture that embraces surplus safety for the elderly.

Before going any further, let me emphasize that there's nothing wrong with a wheelchair or cane or walker, nor is there anything wrong with needing to use one. They're important and necessary aids, and no one should ever be demeaned or diminished if they become necessary. Those who require their use should never be discouraged from using them.

However, resisting their assistance shouldn't be considered a bad thing, as some in the anti-ageism movement would like. Wanting to continue walking without a walker or a wheelchair isn't a futile and dangerous rejection of the truth of aging or the reality of decline.

More than 80 percent of nursing home residents now spend time sitting in a wheelchair every day. While most are placed into wheelchairs to prevent falls, statistics show that up to 25 percent of falls are associated with wheelchair use (Research Gate/American Society of Consult Pharmacist 2007). Wheelchairs also fail miserably in their other supposed benefit of improved mobility, as the majority nursing home residents are unable to propel their own wheelchairs. (Annals of Long-Term Care: Clinical Care and Aging 2010).

In addition, once in a wheelchair, the elderly are usually perceived as being past rehabilitation potential and are overlooked for therapeutic treatment. Wheelchair use then leads very quickly to deconditioning, with a loss of physical function and a loss of independence and autonomy, not to mention a long list of physical issues such as falls, bruises, edema, pressure ulcers, skin tears, nerve impingement and increased incidence of infections.

Residents who no longer walk have a 3.5-times higher risk of developing urinary tract infections, and a 6.6-time higher risk of developing pneumonia than nonusers. (Managed Healthcare Connect/ Prevention of Overuse of Wheelchairs in Nursing Homes, 2010). Entertainment icon Dick Van Dyke, 92, has written a book on the topic called "Keep Moving and Other Tips and Truths about Aging."

"I've seen 90-year-old guys get off their walkers who didn't believe that they could do it," Van Dyke said in his book. "My takeaway is just keep moving! People throw in the towel and stop doing anything, and that's when they start to seize up. I've had arthritis since I was 40, but it doesn't bother me because I stretch and move every day. I get on the treadmill for as long as it feels right. Then I do some resistance and strength training with weights. The main thing is, get on your feet and get interested in something. Be aware of the mind-body connection, because a little blood and oxygen through your brain will change the way you think. And without exercise, you can't do it."

For many of us, there'll come a time when we should — and must — sit down. But in our ageist culture, we're led to believe that the time comes sooner than it actually ought to. Prescribing use of a wheelchair to prevent falls is much easier than prescribing regular functional fitness exercises. And, of course, sitting down is much easier than exercise of any kind.

It's up to each of us to decide how much we want to lean into the challenges of growing older. There's no right or wrong. I can only assure you that — as is the case with all life's challenges — resisting the inertia to stop provides the pathway to keep going.

CHAPTER 17

DESTIGMATIZING DEMENTIA

---

*Overcoming Shame, Discovering Hope
and Celebrating Moments of Joy*

66
—
*Those with dementia are still people and
they still have stories and they still have
character and they are all individuals and
they are all unique. And they just need to
be interacted with on a human level.*
—CAREY MULLIGAN

OUR CULTURE VIEWS AGING AS an unattractive, undesirable and unfortunate tragedy. And since Alzheimer's disease and other forms of dementia are considered aging disorders, the stigma surrounding them is unrelenting. Many who fear that they may have Alzheimer's won't get tested, and many who are newly diagnosed won't talk about it for fear of being ostracized.

Although it's widely misdiagnosed, nearly half of all Americans age 85 and older are estimated to have Alzheimer's, with a new case diagnosed every 66 seconds. By 2050, an estimated 16 million Americans will have the disease, with a new case diagnosed every 33 seconds. Two-thirds of those affected will be women.

If estimates are correct, the economic toll extracted by Alzheimer's alone will be a mind-boggling $1.2 trillion a year by 2050, making it the most expensive health crisis to ever face the nation. It has the potential to singlehandedly bankrupt Medicare and Medicaid. And it will, with complete certainty, bankrupt millions of families. It's easy to see how; the average cost to care for an Alzheimer's patient is nearly $300,000 for the last five years of life.

All dementias are neurodegenerative or progressive illnesses. They're also terminal. Not surprisingly, multiple studies reveal that adults now fear Alzheimer's disease more than cardiac disease or cancer — and the pharmaceutical and nutraceutical industries are all-too-anxious to capitalize on this growing fear.

We're being subtly conditioned to wonder whether every memory lapse is the beginning of a progressive and incurable disease. Memory and brain health nutritional supplements, with little to no scientific evidence of being effective, rack up U.S. sales of more than $3 billion annually, a number that's expected to reach $12 billion by 2024. This is the Machine exploiting your fears.

We're becoming so traumatized by the fear of Alzheimer's that we've begun to jump to the worst possible conclusion whenever we go to the kitchen and forget what we wanted, or whenever we struggle with name recall or word-finding. Sometimes, I think everyone should avoid watching Jeopardy! Under the pressure to answer quickly, the struggle for memory recall is highly exaggerated, leaving us with serious concerns about our cognitive health.

In many ways, Alzheimer's has become the older adult's version of the monster under the bed. And as our parents taught us decades ago, the only way to deal with the monster is to get down on our hands and knees and look for him. We must confront Alzheimer's by learning as much about it as we can. We must improve our lifestyles to reduce or delay our chances of getting it. We must fund the critical research needed to develop therapies to prevent, treat and perhaps even cure it. We must support organizations that serve those who have it. Most of all, we must talk openly about it.

We must overcome the notion that dementia is a disease about which we should feel ashamed. We must replace the old Alzheimer's narrative of fear, hopelessness, isolation, despair and loss with one of hope, possibility, love, connection, purpose and courage. We must begin telling a new story that encourages those diagnosed to focus on their strengths and what they can still do and enjoy, rather than on areas in which they may be experiencing diminishing capabilities.

In truth, there's much to be hopeful about. Our understanding of the disease continues to grow rapidly, and promising new treatments are being tested every day. There's every reason to believe that therapies will someday be developed that will not only slow or prevent the onset of Alzheimer's but could reverse symptoms and perhaps cure it.

As tragic as the loss of memory is, we now know that even those in the advanced stages of Alzheimer's can still experience joy. They crave meaningful daily social connection and have the need to share love. They can still live in the moment. Ironically, isn't that what we're all trying to do anyway?

People with Alzheimer's are still here, just harder to access. It's our job as caregivers to help them experience moments of joy and meaningful human connection. Let the researchers focus on what's wrong or what's gone. Our job is to focus on and celebrate what remains.

That's a powerful and effective strategy for dealing with aging in general. There's always something that can be celebrated, built upon and maintained until it can't be. Then the focus must shift to what remains, which can likewise be celebrated, built upon and maintained until it can't be. Then the focus shifts, once again, to what remains.

Until there are major scientific and medical breakthroughs, we must accept that we can't pull our loved ones back, but we can remain with them in the most meaningful ways. We can provide the encouragement, love and dignity that every human desires and deserves.

Brain Fitness Club

When I learned that the International Council on Active Aging had named the Brain Fitness Club in Winter Park, Florida, one of North America's most innovative active-aging programs, I was anxious to speak with its organizers and perhaps even some if its members.

"All the Brain Fitness Club members have a memory impairment disorder of some sort," said director Peggy Bargmann, a registered nurse specializing in gerontology who has been an innovator in the field of brain health for decades. "They're all in the early stages, so they all know that they have memory impairment and they all want to be here. I'm not sure if they'll want to be interviewed on camera, but I'll ask."

Surprisingly, most were eager to share what they've learned about the disease. "I used to think that I was alone," said Lucy McBean. "And I did more crying than anything else, because I didn't know that other people were going through the same thing. Now I don't feel bad if I don't understand something or I don't remember something. I just say, 'I don't remember.'"

The Brain Fitness Club meets twice weekly for four hours, and topics include everything from nutrition and exercise to the latest therapies and facilitation techniques. The day that we visited, instructor Bob Kodzis was leading members in an improvisation game designed to help overcome fear of failure. "People with memory challenges don't easily forgive themselves for forgetting, and that decreases their quality of life," Kodzis said. "They're so afraid of being wrong, of disappointing their families and friends, that they withdraw. Improvisation teaches them there are no wrong answers. There are no mistakes. It's OK to forget and move on."

Said member Nancy Dulniak: "This is a really safe place to come and be yourself. We've learned not to be afraid of saying the wrong thing or forgetting something, because we all have that problem."

"It's OK to forget" is the gift that we should give all who suffer from Alzheimer's and other forms of dementia. Focusing on what's working and not worrying about or trying to recover what's missing is one of the foundational tenets of the Brain Fitness Club. "We're strictly a capabilities-based program, so we don't look at disability at all," said Bargmann. "We only look at what our members can do, not what they can't do. Instead of a rehab program that takes what's broken and tries to fix it, we focus on what's working well and develop ways to keep doing well at it."

Years ago, one of Bargmann's patients pleaded with her to help destigmatize an Alzheimer's diagnosis. "He said, 'When people hear that I have Alzheimer's disease, they expect me to be in a nursing home drooling, and I'm not. I'm living. I want people to know that you can live with Alzheimer's disease. So please, get out there and stop the stigma that we're living with.' That's been my mission ever since."

Of course, no club will ever remove the fear of an Alzheimer's diagnosis. But I ended our visit with the clear knowledge that those affected still thrive on socialization and human connection. They still enjoy life, and with a little understanding and help they can have a much higher quality of life than we've been led to believe.

We owe it to them, and to ourselves, to remove the stigma associated with all forms of dementia. If we don't, as the cost and the burden of care increases, it will be increasingly easy for our ageist culture to look at those afflicted as simply the unfortunate victims of an incurable disease who are no longer themselves. The Machine will dehumanize them to justify the tragic lack of funding and resources available for their care. "That's life, they had their run" will become the growing cultural chorus of denial.

The odds are overwhelming that every family will have a deeply personal experience with dementia, just as I have.

Tom, Molly, Mom and Dad

I lost both of my parents over an 18-month period in 2011 and 2012, and I certainly wasn't alone. At the time, about 5,000 baby boomers every day were saying goodbye to a parent. That loss is usually gradual, emotional and exhausting. For us, it was all of the above, especially for my sister and brother who lived near my parents in Scottsdale, Arizona.

Both of my parents were among the millions diagnosed with Alzheimer's in their 80s. My father was diagnosed first, and after a few years of gradually worsening symptoms, my mother lost both the desire and the ability to care for him. She, like many older caregivers, was overwhelmed by not only the responsibility but also by the fear that the window was closing on her opportunity to pursue her passions, especially travel, with whatever time she might have left.

With a great sense of guilt, she moved my father into a nearby memory-care home, where he was miserable. All he really wanted out of life was to be in his own home, on the couch, watching sports on television with a beer in one hand and the remote in the other. Now, he woke up every morning in an unfamiliar place, surrounded by "a bunch of old people." He couldn't drink beer and had no control over the television. He called my mother several times a day to complain, which only added to her stress and guilt.

When, at my mother's request, the memory-care home no longer allowed him to make phone calls, he all but imploded and was medicated as a result. For millions of Alzheimer's patients, that's where the story ends. Or at least that's where the meaningful and enjoyable part of life ends. My brother, Tom Middleton, lived nearby. And when he discovered how unhappy, under-stimulated and over-medicated my father was, he literally "broke him out" and took him in to his own home.

Tom knew absolutely nothing about caring for an 85-year-old Alzheimer's patient, but he knew everything about creating and celebrating moments of joy. He knew everything about love and dignity. Unconstrained by accepted protocol for dealing with an Alzheimer's patient, he simply got up every day and helped my father enjoy every moment. They watched sports, drank beer and took in the sights during long drives to nowhere. They sat on Tom's motorcycle in the driveway, took walks and made video phone calls to family and friends. In truth, they lived like a couple of fraternity brothers whose mission in life was simply to chill, enjoy and experience.

Tom didn't fight the disease. He didn't engage in "therapy." He didn't scold Dad when he couldn't remember something that he'd been told just 30 seconds before. He didn't remind him that he had a disease and wasn't as capable as he once was. He didn't quiz him about past events and wasn't agitated by the same questions over and over. He did everything possible to see that Dad wasn't a danger to himself or others. But he also let him make his own choices.

Tom didn't try to bring Dad back. He simply accompanied him on his daily journey and allowed him to live in the moment — without judgment. As a result, Dad experienced great love and joy until he passed away at age 87 from complications unrelated to Alzheimer's.

Unfortunately, by this time my mother was herself in the early stages of Alzheimer's. As she had feared, she was no longer able to travel. And after a couple of minor traffic incidents, she was forced to give up her driver's license. My sister, Molly Middleton Meyer, resigned her teaching position to care for Mother, and the stress quickly took a serious toll. "I wasn't working," Molly recalled. "I was going through a divorce and caring daily for both a child at home and an ailing mother who lived nearby. I grew depressed and hit rock bottom mentally. I got help for my depression, but I needed a lifeline, something that I could do for myself. I asked, 'What am I good at? Where do I feel safe?' The answer came immediately — school. I decided to get a master's degree."

Molly was accepted into the low-residency MFA creative writing program at Lesley University in Cambridge, Massachusetts, where the professors encouraged her to study poetry. Said Molly: "I've always been a writer but had never written a poem. Something made me say, 'What the hell? Why not?'"

As she was preparing to leave for one of her 10-day, on-campus residencies, she received a call from Mother, whose speech was badly slurred: "She said, 'Can you come over? Something's wrong. There's blood everywhere.'" Mother had fallen in the middle of the night, fracturing her skull and suffering a stroke. She was immediately hospitalized and would now require full-time care. Molly called the university and dropped out of the MFA program.

"When I got up the following morning, I felt like I was quitting on myself," she said. "I called the university back and told them everything. I shared my issues and asked if they could be accommodated." Her professors encouraged her to continue. The struggle, they believed, would only make her a better writer.

Mother was moved from the hospital into an acute-care home and then into my brother's home where she passed away within a matter of months. "I lost both parents to Alzheimer's in a relatively short period of time," Molly said. "I couldn't stop thinking about what I'd seen in memory-care centers. I'd become increasingly frustrated with much of their therapy, which I came to believe only dehumanizes those for whom so much is already being lost. I thought about what Tom was able to do for Dad and what I was studying in school. I began to believe in the power of poetry to creatively engage Alzheimer's patients in a fun and dignifying way."

Molly earned her MFA in poetry, read everything she could find on dementia and studied every type of existing therapy. "I found nothing close to what I envisioned," she said. Through trial and error, she developed a process that uses sensory objects and poetry recitation to stimulate memories and flashes of imagination. The results were dramatic and Molly quickly began working with residents in some of the nation's top memory-care homes. "I start with an idea and get the train moving, but you never really know where it's going to end up," she added. "We were writing a poem about the moon recently, and someone thought I said 'mule.' That sparked a memory. So, we were off and running with a poem about mules. Some-times, you just have to jump on board and enjoy the ride."

Within a matter of moments, inspired by a series of prompts and working together as a team, Molly's "poetry patients" write beautiful verse after beautiful verse. "The first time I did this, the caregivers stood there with their mouths open," recalled Molly. "They saw people do and say things that they didn't know were possible. When the hour-long session was finished, they asked, 'How much do you charge, and can you fit us into your schedule?'"

Through her work, Molly joined the growing group of thoughtful and passionate caregivers who are now flipping the rules for interacting with Alzheimer's patients. "We must learn to live in the moment with those that we're caring for, and to make that moment as joyous as possible," she said. "Yes, your relationship changes. But you still have the power to bring joy and meaning and love to their lives. That's what Tom did. Dad experienced a fantastic quality of life because Tom didn't mourn the loss of a father; he celebrated a newfound friend. He only cared about giving Dad the dignity that he deserved. He was willing to go with him on his journey. I wasn't able to do that at the time — but that's exactly what I do now."

Molly's work is a tribute to our parents. "I look in the faces of those I work with and see my mom and dad," she said. "I meet the most amazing people, and it's such a gift to only know them now. I don't know them as people who've lost something. I know them as people who are hungry for stimulation, eager for fun and hungry for love."

Molly is among the growing number of caregivers and health-care providers who are working hard to destigmatize dementia. Scientists and researchers are doing their part to discover how best to treat it. But most importantly, we must do our part. We can have a huge impact on our future cognitive health via the lifestyle choices that we make every day: how we think, what we eat, how much we move, where we live, with whom we socialize, how we learn and how we challenge ourselves. These choices can help delay, prevent and even overcome cognitive decline. There have been countless cases of elderly men and women who showed no outward signs of dementia. But when their brains were examined during autopsies, they were found to be riddled with amyloid plaques and neurofibrillary tangles — the two pathological hallmarks that define Alzheimer's disease. In other words, they were somehow able to overcome the pathology. Most researchers now believe that they did it day by day — one positive lifestyle choice at a time.

CHAPTER 18

THE CHALLENGE OF AGING IN PLACE

Why It Takes a Village

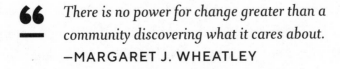

There is no power for change greater than a community discovering what it cares about.
—MARGARET J. WHEATLEY

PERHAPS BECAUSE OF THE FEELING shared by many that moving into a senior-living community is "giving up," there's a nearly universal aspiration to age in place. Ninety percent of all adults over age 65 say they'd prefer to stay in their current residences and live independently for the rest of their lives.

Aging in place sounds great. But it only works if you're plugged into an effective and enthusiastic support community. The notion that we can live until we die without relying on outside assistance is unrealistic. We'll all need help. The quality of that help will, to a large degree, determine the quality of our lives.

We need easy access to resources, services and support that will change as our needs change. We need homes and communities that will do the same. We need regular social and mental stimulation. We need intergenerational connection. We need lifelong learning and volunteer opportunities. We need neighbors who care about us and are willing to assist us. Without all these resources, aging in place is nothing more than a pleasing but implausible concept. In fact, without these resources, aging in place could be more accurately described as dying in place.

It takes a great deal of planning and preparation for aging in place to be successful. So, if 90 percent of us aspire to age in place, why do so few prepare for that eventuality? Why do so few communities invest the time and resources to provide that opportunity?

To many, thinking about aging in place when purchasing a home in their 30s or 40s is akin to wondering how a new dress might someday look in a coffin. But the things that make a home and a community suitable for aging in place are the same things that make them suitable for life at every age.

Aging in place is about universal design, adaptive architecture and easy-to-use technology. It's about social connection and community support. It's about access to wellness and fitness programs, state-of-the-art healthcare and creative stimulation. These are cool, hip, important and powerful trends that are anything but "old" — and they aren't going anywhere.

Our refusal to consider aging in place while we're still young is another manifestation of the Machine and its omnipresent propaganda campaign, working to taint anything that remotely references the challenges of growing older.

Understanding the requirements of aging in place and incorporating them into your life planning doesn't mean that you're ready to withdraw, or that you ever will be. It's the exact opposite. It's a sign that you're going to optimize your future. It's a sign that you're preparing to squeeze every drop out of life for years to come.

Aging is a universally shared experience. Acknowledging its unique challenges in every life stage helps us better prepare for what's next. Forty years ago, most of us never thought about growing older, let alone thought to prepare for it. Thankfully, that's beginning to change — however slowly.

When homebuyers of all ages understand the lasting value — and resale value — of having aging-in-place features incorporated into the design of their homes, then the homebuilding industry will respond with a marketable concept that doesn't feel old, but rather smart. When astute homebuyers understand that aging in place will become a highly desirable option in the years ahead — and that four walls alone can't provide that opportunity — communities will respond with the kinds of programs and resources that will enable residents to remain in their homes.

Every community in the world should aspire to become a community that older residents never want to leave. One of the best examples of a community that gets it and is taking big, bold and even visionary steps to facilitate aging in place is Winter Park, Florida.

At the core of Winter Park's investment in the future of its residents is the Winter Park Health Foundation (WPHF), a private, nonprofit organization that has been working tirelessly since 1994 to make Winter Park one of the healthiest communities in the U.S. — and one of the best places to live for residents of all ages.

The latest and perhaps greatest example of the foundation's vision and commitment is the new, 78,000-square-foot, state-of-the-art Center for Health and Wellbeing. While the center itself is a one-of-a-kind blend of wellness, fitness and medical resources all under one roof, what makes it truly unique is the Wellbeing Network.

The Wellbeing Network is a partnership between the Winter Park Health Foundation and Growing Bolder that operates from a studio within the Center for Health and Wellbeing. Its mission is to celebrate community members who are practicing healthy living and positive aging, and to share what's happening inside the center with those unable to be there in person.

"Through the Wellbeing Network, our vision is to serve the whole community regardless of barriers that may make it difficult for them to visit the center," said Diana Silvey, WPHF vice president. "We're committed to making sure all residents have the opportunity to benefit from the many resources, services and activities offered at the center."

The Wellbeing Network is available online and on an app, making it accessible to everyone, anywhere, on all digital devices. This unique network is an inspirational example of a commitment to aging in place.

You've heard the old African proverb: "It takes a village to raise a child." It can appropriately be modified to: "It takes a village to age in place." More specifically, it takes a village like Winter Park, Florida, and an organization like the Winter Park Health Foundation.

Technology Will Transform Aging in Place

The Wellbeing Network is one example of how technology is dramatically improving the potential for aging in place. Just as the space race spurred technological innovation in the 1960s, the age wave is spurring similar innovation in home technologies, healthcare delivery and the service economy. This innovative technology will completely transform our lives by turning our homes into helpers, healers, companions, caregivers, empowerers and facilitators.

Soon, our homes will have two architectures. One will be the physical design that we see and experience every day; the other will be a nearly invisible set of sensors and connected service providers that will monitor, manage and motivate daily behaviors to support our wellbeing. Our homes will help us quickly and safely navigate both the physical and the online world.

The brain of the intelligent home will be connected to the cloud, facilitating what's called the Internet of Things (IoT). Household objects will use wireless connections to think, talk and communicate with one another and the outside world, dynamically aggregating and managing a wide variety of applications (apps) that impact every aspect of our lives.

Smart toilets, sonogram bathtubs, mirrors that diagnose health issues and an endless array of devices that track and monitor our balance, blood sugar, heart rate, blood pressure, sleep routine, eating habits and more will all be connected to health-management providers via the Internet of Things.

Telehealth will become the standard in healthcare delivery and support, with telecommunication technologies facilitating virtual doctor visits and a wide range of medical, health and educational services through a more convenient and cost-effective system.

The hospital bed of the near future will be in your home, which is a good thing because older adults are prone to complications resulting from confinement in hospitals.

Home-based hospital care will provide in-home treatment for health issues that today usually require acute inpatient care. Multiple studies show that home-based hospital care produces patient outcomes equal to, or better than, in-hospital care — and can lower costs by more than 30 percent over traditional hospitalization.

Three Questions

MIT AgeLabs, part of the world-famous MIT School of Engineering, focuses on solutions to the many challenges of longevity. AgeLabs has developed a simple yet profound exercise based on three questions that can lead to a deeper understanding of not only the basic needs that make life worthwhile, but also the challenges of aging in place or "independent" living.

1. Who Will Change My Light Bulbs?

At some point as we age, climbing a ladder to change a light bulb becomes a very bad idea. Do you want your 88-year-old father changing bulbs in the ceiling? If your mother is living alone, will she try to navigate the ladder or simply live in the darkness to avoid the risk of falling?

"Who will change my light bulbs?" really asks much bigger questions: Do I have a long-term home maintenance plan that will enable me to continue living comfortably and safely at home? Do I live in a community that offers basic maintenance services to older residents living alone? Do I have a network of family and friends that can assist me on a regular basis with chores that I now take for granted?

Eventually, these simple tasks will no longer be possible or advisable for us to perform. And not having a resource for assistance will signal the end of living independently.

2. How Will I Get an Ice Cream Cone?

This question isn't really about an ice cream cone. It's about quality of life. It's about the ability to continue making the kinds of choices and enjoying the everyday activities that we take for granted. It's about the services and the community that surround us.

Asking "How will I get an ice cream cone?" is really asking: Do I have adequate transportation options to go where I want, when I want? When driving is no longer possible, are there readily available and affordable alternatives that will enable me to make the short trips that I want and not just those that I need? Are there businesses nearby that provide the opportunity to have an ice cream cone, watch a movie, go shopping or attend a concert?

3: Who Will I Have Lunch With?

The older we get, the more important social interactions become to our overall health and wellbeing. Even with adequate finances, living alone without a social support circle seriously threatens healthy aging. In fact, low social interaction has the same effect on mortality as smoking 15 cigarettes a day.

Young people age 16 to 24 who are neither employed nor in school are classified as "disconnected youth," and deemed at high risk for depression, sickness, violence and suicide. The same is true for disconnected adults. But once we reach our 70s and 80s, social isolation is viewed more as an unfortunate but acceptable fact of life than as a dangerous and preventable situation.

Today, more than 40 percent of women over age 65 live alone. Consequently, planning where and with whom to retire may be as important as planning for how much it will cost. A retirement home in the mountains may sound appealing. But living in a remote location may mean a life of isolation without an adequate network of friends and the ability to connect with them.

The answer to the question "Who will I have lunch with?" is a good indicator of the strength of your social network — not the social network of "friends" that you might have online, but friends who you see face-to-face on a regular basis. These relationships, and the ability to maintain them, are critical to a healthy and active lifestyle

Active-Adult Communities

For companies in the rapidly growing active-adult or age-restricted community development space, the task is clear and the need is immediate. These communities are no longer places to withdraw and cocoon. They should be viewed as "launch pads to what's next."

The top active-adult communities appear to be in an all-out arms race to offer the best amenities — pools, gyms and even sports bars. While these perks are important, planners and developers should increase their focus on programs that help residents gain the skills necessary to pursue and monetize their passions in the years and decades ahead. These programs should provide opportunities for meaningful and exceptional experience. Younger adults might be interested in collecting Depression glass or movie memorabilia, but older adults are interested in collecting experiences.

Adults age 55 and older are among the most entrepreneurial of all. I've suggested to several active-adult communities that they create an on-campus business incubator in which experts from the community visit regularly to provide guidance on business strategies, writing business plans, raising capital, understanding trademark law and other topics.

Other how-to programs might include monetizing the internet, writing and publishing an e-book, understanding social media, learning Photoshop, joining the gig economy, running a non-profit from your apartment, promoting a blog and marketing on Facebook. Also intriguing would be, for example, an App of the Week Club or a VR/AR (Virtual Reality/ Augmented Reality) Club. The ideas and the opportunities to create meaningful programs that are true differentiators are everywhere.

I feel the most important program of all is "The Art of Growing Bolder." Every senior-living community in the world should be offering some kind of framework for changing belief systems, creating a culture of yes and enabling the pursuit of passion and purpose.

Every community has the potential to be a great place to live. But a successful active-adult or senior-living community can't he isolated from the larger community around it. Seclusion and solitude represent a romanticized vision of retirement that isn't conducive to health or happiness.

Peaceful isolation is something we should pursue on occasion — but it's a terrible prescription for long-term daily living. The best active-adult and senior-living communities provide easy access to everything — groceries, entertainment, dining, intergenerational socialization, volunteer opportunities, public transportation, healthcare, banking services and more. It's all about walkability and connectivity.

CHAPTER 19

A GOOD DEATH

Orchestrating a Loving, Peaceful and Pain-Free Goodbye

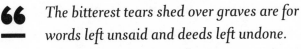

The bitterest tears shed over graves are for words left unsaid and deeds left undone.
—HARRIET BEECHER STOWE

WHILE WE'RE PURSUING A Growing Bolder lifestyle, it's important to always acknowledge the one truth that can't be denied and shouldn't be ignored. That truth is that we're all mortal beings and we're all going to die. I know — major bummer.

Many people, with monastic discipline, lead healthy lifestyles and make all the "right" decisions. And yet, at some point, they begin to decline and then they die. The lucky ones have died quickly and painlessly. But the final result is always the same. We're all taking the same trip.

Since Growing Bolder is about acknowledging the realities of life while maximizing the opportunities of growing older, our focus can't be limited to how we live. It must also include how we die.

If we believe in a hereafter, then every minute that we're alive, until our final breath, is an opportunity to prepare for what's next. If we don't believe in a hereafter, then every minute that we're alive, until our final breath, is an opportunity to experience the significance and joy that we'll never have again.

None of us will get out of here alive. But with a little planning and preparation, we can dramatically increase the chance that we'll get out of here in a peaceful, painless and loving way that eases our transition to whatever's next and comforts those we love.

Tragically, few of us are willing to even acknowledge death's unavoidable existence, much less spend time talking about it. To ignore our mortality is to depreciate the value of the gift that we've been given. Death awareness dramatically increases life appreciation. Obsessing about death is unhealthy, but ignoring its reality is an equally flawed strategy. Technology, modern medicine and positive lifestyle modification might delay death

— but nothing will stop it. It could come today, tomorrow or in 10,000 days. But it's coming.

The mere thought of death has saddened, confounded, terrorized, frustrated and discouraged most of us since we were children. I can remember waking up in the middle of the night when I was a young boy and thinking about death. Or trying not to think about it. I really don't know which.

I vividly remember the strange and uneasy feeling. Time slowed down. It was as though the darkness and silence of the night were not just encouraging me to think about death, they were demanding it. I'd give it the attention it demanded for a few minutes, but even at age 4 or 5 — or perhaps *especially* at age 4 or 5 — it was the ultimate mind boggler. I soon had to escape to thoughts about going to the beach or my upcoming birthday party.

I don't wake up in the middle of the night thinking about death any more. But I do occasionally think about it during the day. The thoughts don't force their way into my consciousness as they did decades ago. I invite them in, because I believe it's foolhardy to ignore an inevitable event that will impact me — in the most direct way imaginable — and everyone I care about.

Preparing for death is as much an opportunity as it is a responsibility. Preparation can save frustration, money and heartache. It can prevent chaos and misunderstanding. It can provide peace of mind to ourselves and our loved ones.

How do we approach death from a Growing Bolder perspective? What's the most positive and powerful way to transition from this life to what's next? The broad strokes are easy. I love living, have no plans to check out before it's my time and am committed to making the sometimes-difficult lifestyle choices that provide the best chance of living a long, active life followed by a short, peaceful death.

I'll most assuredly rage against the dying of the light — not for as long as is possible but for as long as is appropriate. I'll fight with every fiber of my being until it's time to surrender. Hopefully, I'll know when that time arrives. Medical science has become adept at prolonging death under the guise of preserving life.

I'll make my wishes known. I'll say the things I would regret not having said. I'll do the things I would regret not having done. I've tried to live my life without being controlled by fear. So, I hope that I'm able to embrace my transition in the same spirit.

Defining A Good Death

I was having a cup of coffee with the director of a hospice organization when she mentioned "a good death." What? A good death? I was fascinated to learn the definition from her perspective.

A good death is one in which we die at home or at a place of our choosing. We're pain-free and surrounded by loved ones. We may have fought death for months or even years, but we've now realized that the fight is over. We've not only accepted the fact that death is approaching, we've embraced it and are ready for it. We're at peace and, in some cases, even filled with wonder and a spirit of curiosity about what's next. Although we may drift in and out of consciousness, we're calmly attended to with love and encouragement.

I believe that the encouragement part is especially important. A good death doesn't include loved ones dramatically imploring the dying to keep on fighting. It's just the opposite. Now is the time to accept and surrender to the fate that no one escapes. Now is the time to feel and express deep gratitude for the blessing of one another and the time spent together.

A good death is a loving, peaceful, pain-free and hopeful goodbye. A good death is embraced with courage and a deep sense of appreciation for having shared the gift of life. There are, of course, tears at a good death. But they're mostly tears of joy and gratitude — not for what's being lost but for what *has been*, and for what *might be*.

A good death delivers a peaceful transition to the deceased and a powerful, uplifting sense of closure to the survivors. There are no regrets.

We do an amazing job of giving our pets good deaths. They're rarely subjected to the frantic, invasive and toxic interventions to which we often subject ourselves and our loved ones. Somehow, when our beloved pets are involved, we're able to determine that it's time. They're comforted with kindness and reassured by the sounds of their loved ones' voices as they slowly drift away. It's tragic that we should have to aspire to a death as peaceful and as well orchestrated as that which we routinely provide our pets.

Death with dignity and with a freedom of expression should be a fundamental human right.

Death is viewed as a failure by the healthcare industry, and that attitude has helped inform our cultural view of dying. Dr. Atul Gawande, in his thought-provoking book "Being Mortal," describes the frantic efforts to keep the frail elderly alive when they are rushed to the hospital following cardiac or respiratory failure. Doctors, of course, do what they've been trained to do. They launch desperate — even manic — efforts to keep such patients breathing and technically alive. Many times, doctors know little to nothing about the history, condition or wishes of elderly people who've been rushed to an emergency room. They only know that he or she is crashing, and it's their job to prevent it. When you're a hammer, everything looks like a nail. The last place most of us want to end up in our final days is an emergency room looking like a nail to a roomful of hammers.

Dr. Gawande describes a team of dedicated professionals injecting, cutting, pumping and pounding on a weak, diseased and brittle body in a desperate attempt to resuscitate at all costs. When the patient mercifully and belatedly dies, the doctors step back, look around the room and then at one another — humiliated at the chaos they created and the trauma they inflicted. This is not a good death.

Hospice has provided care, usually at home, to those nearing the end of life for nearly 40 years. Its work is universally praised. But it remains significantly under-utilized because it's viewed by many as a sign of defeat. Ironically, those who enter hospice live, on average, longer than those with similar conditions who don't receive hospice care. At some point, the process of giving in and embracing the end is more restorative than continuing to fight.

Hospice care shouldn't be equated with giving up. It should be viewed as a life-enhancing pathway to a peaceful and painless passing at home — the kind of death that everyone says they want, but few mange to achieve. Statistics reveal that 80 percent of Americans say they would strongly prefer to die at home. However, 60 percent of all Americans die in acute-care hospitals while 20 percent die in nursing homes. Only 20 percent realize the ideal of dying at home.

By the way, the number one reason more people don't want to die at home is because they believe their death will place a burden on family members. Research proves the exact opposite to be true. Grief and stress, it turns out, are less intense for relatives of people who die at home.

So how do we close the gap between preference and reality? How can we increase our chances of having a "good death?"

We know that the mortality rate is 100 percent. Yet, we choose to ignore the inevitable. Tragically, only half of all Americans have discussed their end-of-life wishes, and only one-third have expressed those wishes in advance directives — a written statement of a person's wishes regarding medical treatment, often including a living will, made to ensure those wishes are carried out should the person be unable to communicate them to a doctor.

Having an advance directive can help avoid a chaotic and violent death under the harsh lights of a cold and impersonal operating room surrounded by strangers beating on our bodies instead of loved ones comforting our souls. There's simply no good reason not to have an advance directive that reflects your current thinking about end-of-life care.

A stunning example that underscores our cultural reluctance to address mortality is the fact that only 44 percent of hospice healthcare workers have completed their own advance directives, according to a study published in the American Journal of Medicine. Astonishingly, these are the very people who have had front-row seats to the struggle, stress and heartache endured by the families of those without advanced directives.

The National Hospice and Palliative Care Organization has a program called CaringInfo.org that offers free, state-specific forms to help us make decisions about end-of-life care before a crisis forces the issue or shifts the responsibility for decision-making to others. It's a quick and simple process, and we can change our directives if we change our minds.

The failure to think about and prepare for death is related to our mania to fight for life, even when that fight is futile. I'm not suggesting that a 40-year-old diagnosed with Stage 4 cancer shouldn't try everything possible to survive. But an 88-year-old with multiple incurable pathologies and disabilities is another matter. Invasive and toxic interventions hold zero hope of curing and restoring a person of that age, and in that condition, to a vibrant life. Nonetheless, if they aren't stopped, doctors will continue treating and prolonging life well beyond the point of patient awareness.

This is what our "modern" healthcare system does. It generates a nearly unstoppable force of medical treatment and intervention designed to prolong life at all costs. Swift deaths are increasingly uncommon. Doctors have a wide range of expensive and invasive tools, technologies and medicines that can keep us alive — but with no quality of life — even after death is certain. And they'll not hesitate to use every tool at their disposal.

Doctors aren't the solution to this crisis. They're the cause. The healthcare system plays into our desire to live forever. If we wait for doctors to tell us there's nothing more they can do, then we'll most assuredly die in the hospital with toxic drugs in our veins and tubes plugged into every orifice. There's a time to be aggressive in the treatment of disease and a time to surrender to mortality with grace and dignity. We're not very good at determining where that line is drawn.

Once again, the problem is culture. And cultural change will come too slowly for you and me. Growing Bolder isn't just about learning how to live, but also learning how to die. We must learn to seize the opportunities and minimize the challenges of life at every stage — including the final one. We must determine — and then demand — the kind of end-of-life care that we, as individuals, desire.

Many people who have terminal illnesses reach a point at which they say: "I'm done. I'm ready." They've decided that the pain they must endure — and the physical, emotional and financial toll required to keep fighting — outweighs their desire to remain alive. Their quality of life has rapidly decreased and there's no hope of ever regaining the mobility, autonomy and vitality that had made waking up in the morning worthwhile.

Shouldn't these people be able to say: "The pain is too much, the loss is too great, the expense is too high and I'm ready to go"? Shouldn't they be able to die at home in a peaceful transition that becomes a celebration of life, instead of in an emergency room fighting a violent and losing battle?

When the very old who are in declining health take a turn for the worse, the knee-jerk reaction is to call 911 and rush them to the hospital. In truth, most elderly people don't want anything to do with hospitals. But if they haven't made their wishes known, that's exactly where they'll end up. And, as thousands of families learn every day, getting out of the hospital is far more difficult than getting in.

As soon as the stretcher rolls through the emergency room doors, the healthcare machine kicks into high gear. And before a patient can say, "I'm not sure I want to become a human pincushion," a battery of expensive and invasive tests have been performed and the examining room has been filled to bursting with mechanical ventilators, electrical defibrillators, dialysis machines, intravenous feeding tubes, medicine bags and a morphine drip — just in case. Surgeons, in the meantime, are plotting the most effective intervention to buy time before launching a more orchestrated assault on the disease processes attacking multiple organ systems in a barely conscious 90-year-old.

Amy Cameron O'Rourke, founder and president of the Cameron Group, has worked for decades in healthcare, specializing in aging and caregiving. A regular contributor to Growing Bolder, O'Rourke cautions families not to get caught up in the all-but-unstoppable momentum of emergency and critical care.

"If you or your loved one ends up in the hospital, slow everything down," she said. "Don't get pushed into making immediate decisions. If the doctor says, 'We must do this test,' reply that you need a few minutes to think and to talk to your family. Buy some time, because it's very easy to get swept up in the moment. Ask yourself, 'If this test detects a medical problem, are we going to do what they recommend?' If the answer is no, then you don't want the test. If there's a brain tumor, are you going to subject an 88-year-old to brain surgery? Or is it better to take him home, keep him comfortable and let him enjoy what time he might have left? It's important to be very frank with physicians. Demand that they talk to you simply as your doctor, not from the hospital liability or physician liability perspective."

This is how 80 percent of Americans end up dying in hospitals or nursing homes when 80 percent would strongly prefer to die at home. They get swept up in medical procedures from which they never recover.

In our final days, almost all of us want to be at home with family and friends, mentally aware and without pain or suffering. That's pretty much it. Our healthcare system has proven itself to be woefully inept at delivering those priorities and helping us achieve what's most important to us at the end of our lives.

As a result, we must be proactive and have conversations with our loved ones about our end-of-life wishes. We must accept the reality of our mortality and be strong enough to know when it's time to surrender. We mustn't get caught up in a hospital death trap that pushes us into oblivion and delirium.

This is a precious, important and valuable time. We must embrace the opportunity of our impending transition to say what needs to be said, to reaffirm our beliefs and priorities, to give thanks for the gifts we've received, to acknowledge our shortcomings, and to release our attachment to worldly possessions and desires. The goal is not to simply bear the unbearable thought of death, but to celebrate the amazing gift of life.

It takes a little planning and a lot of luck to achieve a good death — but it's a goal worth aspiring to. Unfortunately, for most of us the strategy for dealing with the reality of death is to simply ignore it until it's sprung upon us. When that happens, we have by default relinquished control to the Machine and tossed our final days, our finances and the mental health of our loved ones into chaos.

Simply saying that we must plan better and prepare more is not enough because we know that a vast majority will neither hear nor heed this advice. The reality is that the unalterable demographic wave is delivering an ever-increasing number of men and women to life's final stage and a vast majority are facing what can be a frightening and traumatic time alone.

Thankfully, there is now a slowly growing movement led by social workers and dedicated volunteers to meet this important need. These so-called death doulas, doulas for the dying, end-of-life coaches or transition guides are filling an important and unmet need by providing compassion and companionship.

End-of-life doulas are nonmedical professionals trained to deliver physical, psychological, emotional and spiritual support to both patients and families. Their purpose is to relieve the stress of facing the end stage of life alone — to assist the passage from this world to the next. They facilitate opportunities for the dying to connect more deeply with loved ones. They create the Growing Bolder opportunity to focus on possibility rather than limitation. To celebrate what remains rather than mourn what has been lost. To find the joy and purpose in life's final days.

If you're looking for an opportunity, if you want to help meet a growing need that can be profoundly rewarding, consider becoming an end-of-life doula. One of the larger and better-known training groups is the International End of Life Doula Association (INELDA) founded in 2015. This is a movement that must grow exponentially to meet a need that is already growing exponentially.

We all must make peace with the impermanence of life. Death is a reality that we must embrace — and the very reason that every second of life is precious. Preparing for death doesn't invite it. In fact, just the opposite. Preparing for death is paying the ultimate respect to life. "It's the knowledge of death that gives meaning to life," said world-renowned geriatrician Dr. Bill Thomas. "Research shows that people who are aware of and embrace their own mortality are happier than people who live with the illusion that they're going to somehow live forever."

CHAPTER 20

THE ART OF THE GROWING BOLDER COMEBACK

A Playbook for Active Longevity

> 66
> *You are never too old to set another*
> *goal or to dream a new dream.*
> —C.S. LEWIS

WE'LL ALL EXPERIENCE AN ENDLESS SERIES of setbacks as we grow older. We'll arrive at countless intersections at which our desires collide with our fears. Do we stretch, trying to move forward? Or do we withdraw, trying to avoid further exposure? These are critical and ultimately life-defining moments that test our wills and our belief systems about what's possible.

Learning how to push through intersections and bounce back from setbacks is one of the most important life skills that we can acquire. Because comebacks, or at least the need for them, are part of the human condition.

This is one of the most important goals of the Growing Bolder mission — to share what's possible. It wasn't long ago that, for an elderly person, a hip fracture was virtually a death sentence, with an 80 percent mortality rate. Patients were treated with a cast, traction and six months of bed rest.

Total hip replacements with complete recovery are now commonplace, even for the elderly. Today, the mortality rate is less than 1 percent for patients under age 80 and only 5 percent for patients over age 90.

I spoke at a caregiving conference about "The Power of Relatable Examples" and on how Growing Bolder tries to smash destructive stereotypes or false narratives by showing what's possible for ordinary people. After I spoke, a caregiver told me about her friend's vibrant, energetic 90-year-old mother, who had broken her hip. Despite their best efforts, she told me, they had been unable to reignite her passion for life. "Honey," the elderly woman had said, "no one comes back from a broken hip at my age." Two months later she was gone.

This is exactly why we need to produce and share the stories of 90-year-olds who *do* come back from hip replacements or spinal reconstructions or organ transplants. It's difficult, if not impossible, for most of us to achieve something that we don't truly believe is possible for ordinary people.

All of us are in the middle of a comeback right now — some more challenging than others. We're coming back from being fired or laid off, from a pulled muscle or a broken back. We're coming back from a bad investment, a bad accident, a bad childhood or a bad relationship. We're coming back from a 48-hour case of the flu or a yearlong battle with cancer. We're coming back from a stroke, a heart attack or a devastating diagnosis.

We're all in the ring, battling life's never-ending challenges — and every challenge represents an opportunity to either make a comeback or to gradually become weaker before eventually giving up. Make no mistake about it: Life will continue to knock us down and the Machine will continue trying to count us out. The only question is this: Will we stand up and fight for all that life still has to offer, or will we accept defeat and stay down?

How successful we are in bouncing back and moving forward has a cumulative effect on how quickly we age, how long we maintain our independence and, ultimately, the overall quality of our lives moving forward.

I'll grant you that it is far easier to buy into the popular and flawed belief that beyond a certain age it's too late to stage a comeback, chart a new course, master a new skill, find new happiness or achieve new success. Comebacks can be difficult and frustrating. If you want to accept your current situation or the impact of your most recent setback, that's your right. But understand that there'll be another setback and then another and then another. Understand that each setback will extract a toll on your overall wellbeing — and the quality of your life will be progressively diminished.

At some point, if we live long enough, nearly all of us will lose the desire to keep fighting and we'll eventually surrender. Not only is there nothing wrong with that, it's an important and appropriate response. But if we don't fully understand the benefits of continuing to mount comebacks for as long as possible, it becomes easy to rationalize giving up years before it's necessary to do so.

Therefore, the next question is: When is it too late to mount a Growing Bolder comeback?

Is it Too Late?

The question arrives in an infinite variety of ways: a glance in the mirror, a bittersweet memory, a comment from a friend or spouse, a few extra pounds on the scale or a few deep breaths at the top of the steps. Has the best part of life really passed? Is it too late to dream and achieve? Is it too late to connect with the passion and purpose that everyone possesses but most have buried in the past?

The answer to this question is informed by decades of seeing older people portrayed as weak and frail. "Help, I've fallen and I can't get up" is designed to put fear into every older person. It discourages risk-taking and reinforces the demeaning and negative stereotyping so prevalent in our culture. Eventually, even walking to the mailbox becomes something to fear. What if I fall? What if I have a heart attack? For most of us, the list of "what ifs" continues to grow exponentially with each year — ultimately keeping us on the couch, paralyzed with fear.

As we age, our comfort zones typically become smaller and smaller. If you find comfort in the status quo, if you prefer what is to what might be, you should probably stop reading right now. This is your red pill/blue pill moment.

Do you want to continue living under the Machine's control, believing that it's too late for you? Or do you want to see how deep the rabbit hole goes? Do you want the life-transforming truth about possibility and opportunity — fully understanding that you must work for it and that nothing is guaranteed?

If so, here are the keys to a Growing Bolder comeback — a playbook for active longevity.

1. Change Your Belief System About Aging

Before you think, "I'm too old, too slow, too weak or too tired," remember that whatever we put into our minds, we also put into our bodies. Stereotypes are internalized, and perceptions become reality. If we believe negative aging stereotypes, we'll quickly become them. Don't worry about getting old. Worry that you believe getting old is a bad thing.

Our future success is largely dependent upon our ability to change our belief system about aging.

Dr. Ellen Langer, a social psychologist at Harvard University, has conducted two fascinating studies on the power of our belief systems: the Counterclockwise study and the Chambermaid study.

In the Counterclockwise study, a group of 80-year-old men spent a week in what Dr. Langer and her colleagues called a "timeless retreat." Half of the men lived in a house that reflected, in every way imaginable, life as it was 20 years before. "The TV and radio programs, the furnishings, the books and all the props in the house were from 20 years earlier," she said. "The men were instructed to live the entire week as if they were actually 20 years younger. They weren't allowed to bring up any events that happened after that period, and they had to refer to themselves, their families and their careers as they were at that time."

The comparison group lived in a normal house. They were instructed to live in the present but *reminisce* about the past. Amazingly, in just one week, the group that lived as though they were in the past experienced marked improvement in their hearing, eyesight, memory, dexterity and appetite compared to those who just reminisced. Most of the limits we assume to be real are simply the result of our mindset. If we can change our mindset, we can change the way we age.

Langer's Chambermaid study was equally revealing. "We took a group of chambermaids and asked them all how much they exercise," Langer said. "They all said they did no exercise at all because they were too busy working and couldn't afford a gym membership. We explained to half of the group that their work was, in fact, exercise. We demonstrated how pushing a vacuum, scrubbing tubs and changing sheets mimicked exercise routines and provided a full-body workout."

After six weeks, the people who were told that their work was, in fact, exercise lost weight, lowered their blood pressure, improved their waist-to-hip ratio and lowered their body-mass index. The only thing that changed was their belief system about what they did. When they thought of it as exercise and not just work, they experienced the benefits of exercise. The people in the control group, who were not told that their work was exercise, experienced none of the health benefits despite doing the same type and amount of work.

What the mind believes, the body embraces. Perceptions determine reality. Our bodies are, in fact, thought transformation machines. We're the shape-shifters written about in science fiction — except that we're not science fiction. What we believe and what we focus on is what we create. It's an infallible law of human existence.

2. Start Today

The one and only day to begin a comeback and start transforming your future is today. Any other day is procrastination and sets you up for near-certain failure. It means that you lack the motivation to start and the willpower to continue.

If we're honest with ourselves, most of us are just treading water. Treading water keeps us alive — for now. It enables us to keep breathing, but it consumes an increasing amount of energy and doesn't move us anywhere. It doesn't solve a problem or create a path forward. It's simply marking time or, at best, buying time. This strategy may work if the Coast Guard has been dispatched. Unfortunately, in life, there's no rescue crew on the way. We can only tread water for so long, and eventually we'll go under. Today is the day to start swimming for shore — even if we can't see it and don't know in which direction to swim.

What's most important to you? What do you care most about? What really matters? Pursue that and forget the rest. We learn this lesson every time we talk to people who have faced major life-threatening challenges. We also learn it from elderly people who are nearing the end of their lives. They all come to realize the value of every moment, because the clock is ticking. Life is precious, and relationships are priceless.

What do you care about? Pursue that and carpe the shit out of this diem.

3. Take a Leap of Faith and Then Take Another

The first step is always the hardest. It's the single step that most people can't take and the single reason that most people never achieve their dreams. Success is, more than anything else, an act of faith. So at some point, we must take a leap of faith. Calculated, strategic risk-taking has always been, and will always be, the path to success — especially as we age.

One of the most exciting and empowering realizations is that the universe supports honest and honorable efforts toward self-improvement. Wanting more life, more abundance and more significance is a biological imperative that's supported by all of creation. Conversely, if we don't exert that level of intent, the universe will push us around. Circumstances that have nothing to do with us will ultimately control our lives. We'll be buffeted about by chance and the impact of random events. We might get lucky. Who knows? We might also win the Publishers Clearing House sweepstakes — but we probably shouldn't spend too much time waiting on the mail carrier.

I've come to believe that life is a series of leaps. Or should be. The good news is, the more leaps we take, the less frightening those leaps become. That's because we've learned that the universe will catch us, provided we're leaping for the right reasons. In other words, the universe likely won't catch you if you're leaping from mentoring underprivileged children to selling them cocaine. But the cops probably will.

Be bold, and mighty forces will come to your aid. Journalist Frank Scully said it best: "Why not go out on a limb? Isn't that where the fruit is?"

4. Don't Be a Wannabe

Almost everyone wants to do something important, exciting or meaningful. Except they don't *really* want to because it's too difficult and requires too great a commitment. Most people who say that they want to help the less fortunate, write a book, run a marathon, lose 75 pounds or stop smoking aren't willing to make the sacrifices necessary to achieve those goals. They love the fantasy but trip over the reality. They have the vision but lack the commitment.

Wannabes satisfy their need to feel as though they're going to do something important by telling others about it and then getting back on the couch. Of course, the initial rush of faux accomplishment quickly subsides, and the wannabe must come up with something else to pretend that he or she is going to do.

We all know wannabes. They become a bit like the boy who cried wolf. We smile and nod, but we don't really believe them when they tell us about their plans. That lack of belief, if it's obvious, makes it more likely that the wannabe is going to remain a wannabe. When we tell others that we're pursuing something important, we want them to believe it. We need them to believe it. There's great power in that belief.

If I tell you that I'm going to do something, and you don't believe it, at best I get nothing back from you. At worst you discourage, mock or dismiss me. That disapproval is all that's needed to stop a wannabe from trying because, more than anything else, wannabes are defined by fear. However, if you sincerely believe in me, my belief in myself grows. My fear decreases while my confidence and determination rise. Wannabes never receive the important benefit of belief from others and ultimately become neverbes.

5. Eliminate the Option Not To

Once you've wrestled with the wannabe beast and decide to do something, eliminate the option to not do that thing.

I swam in college, but after graduation didn't swim a lap for nearly 35 years. Inspired by many of the people whom we feature on Growing Bolder, I decided to start swimming again.

The only group workout near my home is at 5:00 a.m. in an outdoor pool. So, I set my alarm for 4:44 a.m. and I'm up immediately and out my door. No snooze button, no "it's too cold," "it's raining or "I got to bed too late and the extra sleep is more important." At 4:44 a.m., our weak selves, programmed by the Machine, become great negotiators. Our weak selves want to engage in a debate about the pros and cons of getting out of bed. Our weak selves will present endless reasons to roll over and remain in bed rather than dive into a swimming pool to work out.

It can be 34 degrees, raining and thundering. But I don't allow myself to ever think, "They'll probably cancel practice." When my alarm goes off, I get up and I go. Period. Admittedly, there've been a few times when I was the only one who showed up, and I had to return home. But eliminating the option of not showing up is the only pathway to a successful comeback.

It's also the easiest pathway. Constantly battling with negative voices in our heads — put there by the Machine — is an exhausting and stress-filled struggle. The voices will question our reasoning and even our sanity. The more we listen to them the stronger they become. Deciding to do something isn't enough. We must eliminate the option to not do it.

6. Develop a Beginner's Mindset, Take Risks and Embrace Failure

As we age we have to resist the urge to regress into that which is comfortable and familiar. To be afraid to fail is to be afraid to live. Don't sit back. Lean into life. Find your passion and pursue it. And don't stop if you fail, which you probably will. Everyone does, at least at first.

Refine, adjust and try again. And again. The only question that matters is this one: How many times are we willing to fail before we succeed? Thomas Edison made at least 1,000 unsuccessful attempts before inventing the light bulb. Someone once asked him, "Isn't it a shame that with the tremendous amount of work you have done you haven't been able to get any results?" That friend reported that "Edison turned on me like a flash, and with a smile replied: 'Results! Why, man, I have gotten a lot of results! I know several thousand things that won't work.'"

I opened a talk recently by saying that I can't wait for my next failure. That statement was met with chuckles and quizzical looks. I explained that I wouldn't be trying something new unless I thought it would enhance my life. And even if that turned out to be true, I'd most likely fail at it initially. Almost no one is good at something new right away — even if it's something that they were "born to do."

We learn and grow by trying, failing and persisting. It's been that way from the moment we took our first breaths. How many times did you hit the side of your face or chin with a spoon before you finally found your mouth? How many times did you fall and get back up before you walked into the outstretched arms of Mommy or Daddy? Life is still offering us its outstretched arms — but we must be willing to fall and get back up to reach its grasp.

Those who ultimately become good at something are simply those who were OK with being bad at it for a while. If we can't deal with failure, we'll never know success. The key is to develop a beginner's mind, which is open to new ideas and possibilities and understands that failure is nothing more than feedback. A beginner's mindset is what opens the door to continued growth and expanded opportunity.

Three-time Olympic gold medalist and Growing Bolder contributor Rowdy Gaines says: "To me, Growing Bolder is about never giving up even if it takes a while to discover what you love or what you're good at. I didn't start swimming until I was a junior in high school, and that's because I had already failed in five different sports: football, baseball, basketball, golf and tennis. I tried out for all and I was cut from all. I never gave up, and neither should you. It doesn't matter if you're 17 or 87. So get out there and take some chances — and remember that you never really fail until you stop trying."

Go forward without fear, with the understanding that our greatest weakness lies in giving up. The most certain way to succeed is always to try just one more time. And every time we try, we must believe. Belief, or lack of belief, will ultimately determine our success or failure. As the great entrepreneur Henry Ford said: "Whether you believe you can do a thing or not, you are right."

7. Increase Your Social Circle, But Nix the Naysayers

We're social animals who need to engage and contribute. Our self-esteem is closely tied to social roles, and the loss of these roles due to retirement and isolation can be devastating. When we're separated from the herd, when we have no one with whom to engage, we decline very rapidly. Dozens of studies have proven that social relationships have a profound influence on mental and physical health, mortality risk and longevity. That's because there's a natural tendency for health-related attitudes, both positive and negative, to spread throughout social networks.

If we're determined to eat a healthier diet, that effort will benefit our spouses and those in our social circles. Conversely, obesity increases substantially for those who have obese spouses or obese friends. Any former drug or alcohol abuser will tell you that they had to remove themselves from the influence of users before getting sober.

Multiple studies, including at Harvard University and the London School of Economics, have consistently identified the source of true happiness as having meaningful relationships. While it's important to remain socially engaged, it's just as important that we pick our friends wisely. When we're teens, peer pressure leads us to do things that we shouldn't. When we're older, peer pressure prevents us from doing things that we should.

Who we spend time with is, ultimately, who we become. Entrepreneur and author Jim Rohn famously said that we're the average of the five people with whom we spend the most time. As we age, that group typically becomes less diverse and more disconnected. If our five people are afraid, pessimistic, inactive, needy, unengaged and unhealthy, then it will be nearly impossible for us to adopt a Growing Bolder lifestyle.

Passion, enthusiasm and optimism are success magnets — the contagious cornerstones of a successful and healthy life. They can make up for experience when we're younger and overcome age bias when we're older. We must surround ourselves with those who share our enthusiasm for life, because no attitude is as potentially harmful as a negative belief system about aging. While the power of positive thinking is well documented, far less attention has been given to the power of negative thinking.

Research reveals that negative begets negative far more than positive begets positive. While positive thinking alone won't ensure the success of any personal comeback or reinvention, negative thinking alone will quickly doom it. Negative thinking leads directly to anxiety, depression, low self-esteem, lack of self-confidence, unhealthy behaviors and, ultimately, sickness. As we begin to encounter the challenges of age, positivity is important. But avoiding negativity is crucial.

There's an ever-increasing group of active, passionate, engaged "seniors" who talk about opportunity instead of disability. They're the age disruptors. Find them and hang out with them as if your life depended on it. Because it does.

Ditch the Debbie Downers, sad sacks and energy vampires. Where you see opportunity and adventure, those influenced by the Machine will see only risk, frivolity and a potentially negative impact on their hyper-cautious lives. Many will suggest that your efforts are a foolish waste of time or money. The possibility of your successful comeback threatens their rationalization that they're doing the best they can do. Mark Twain said: "Keep away from people who try to belittle your ambitions. Small people always do that, but the really great make you feel that you, too, can become great."

There's little that's better for overall health than a happy and supportive marriage. But there's little that's worse for overall health than a stressful and unhappy marriage. Research reveals that the negative effect of marital strain on health becomes even greater with advancing age. If you're committed to discovering the power, passion and possibility of aging, and your spouse can only see loss and limitation, then your comeback will be difficult, if not impossible.

8. Reconnect with the Muscle Memory of Youth

Everyone remembers the struggle, the focus and especially the falls endured while learning to ride a bicycle. It wasn't easy until, suddenly, it was. But once we learn, it's with us forever. Even if we haven't ridden a bicycle in decades, we can jump back on and ride immediately. That's another kind of muscle memory — different from the kind mentioned in Chapter 12.

Of course, our muscles don't really have memory. But our brains do a remarkable job of storing and recalling the thousands of sophisticated associated movements required to perform certain tasks — such as riding a bike. Using computer storage as an analogy, all the movements associated with this activity are stored as a single file labeled "ride a bike." When we hop on a two-wheeler, our brains instantaneously access that file, download the entire program and off we go.

What makes this even more remarkable — and even more exciting — is that the feelings we have experienced while participating in the activity are stored in the very same file. And the feelings return as quickly as the movements themselves. It's highly complex yet exquisitely simple. It's an amazing resource that we all have at our disposal.

So, what do you know how to do that will activate previously stored sequences and emotions? Did you learn to paint, juggle, swim, sing, tap dance, write poetry or create pottery? If you learned to do almost anything through practice, the muscle memory is still stored in your brain and can be accessed to jumpstart and accelerate your comeback.

For me, it was swimming. When I returned to the sport after a 35-year absence, not only did I still have muscle memory, I had emotional memory. I immediately reconnected with feelings of strength, speed, success, determination and commitment. It took one lap back in the pool to begin short-circuiting the Machine.

I often wonder if I'd enjoy swimming as much today if I hadn't stayed away from the sport for so many years. I wonder if that positive emotional attachment to the sport would have gradually declined if I'd kept on swimming. I don't have an answer for that. But I do know what the Machine wanted me to believe: You're too old for this stuff. You'll just embarrass yourself.

When I came back, perhaps naively, I expected to swim like I did decades ago. Surprisingly, I did. In a very short time, I was a member of six world-record-setting relay teams. I'd set two Pan American records and won seven individual national championships in my age group.

One of the standard pieces of advice to older people is: "Don't live in the past." I've come to believe that we take that advice far too literally. Of course, staying in your room and thinking only about the past won't lead to any new adventures. But reconnecting with your past as a means of informing your present and inspiring your future can be a very powerful technique.

When we interviewed 101-year-old Julia "Hurricane" Hawkins after she set a world age-group record in the 100-meter dash, she shared the story of her 70-year marriage. "We were married on the phone because he was at Pearl Harbor when it was bombed, and it was another year before he got back home," she said. "During that year, he wrote me nearly every day. I have many wonderful letters that I received when I was just 20. I started re-reading them last year, and I immediately began feeling young again. Maybe that's why I started running at age 100."

Have you seen the videos of men and women with advanced Alzheimer's disease who are totally non-communicative until headphones are placed over their ears and music from their youth is played? They sit upright, smiles spread across their faces, and they begin to move to the music. Many even talk for the first time in years. After living in a world in which nothing is familiar, a song from decades ago is instantly recognized, providing immediate joy and a surge of energy.

You don't want to live in the past. But you should plan on stopping by for a visit every now and then.

9. Ready, Fire, Aim

More businesses are now adopting a general strategy that for decades was used as an example of what *not* to do — the Ready, Fire, Aim method. Instead of knowing exactly how a new product or service will be received, these businesses launch products as early as possible and then rapidly adjust as the market provides direction. It's a faster path to a better product.

Ready, Fire, Aim is the perfect prescription for discovering your passions and engaging in this new life stage. Try anything that's even remotely interesting. Say yes to social engagements that you might otherwise have blown off. Once you're off the couch and engaged in life, you'll be exposed to people, activities and opportunities that you didn't know existed. Then you can zero in on what interests you the most.

If you don't know who you are or what you love. Act. Action will reveal the answers.

10. Find and Learn From "Someone Like Me, Only Better"

Not long ago, if you were disabled, suffered from a disease, had a physical, emotional or mental issue of any kind or were simply beyond a certain age, there were likely no role models in your community to show by example what was possible.

One of the greatest benefits of the internet is that it has the power to connect us with others who are like us. The result is the empowering realization that this person is "like me, only better." Not a better person, or a more worthwhile person — just someone who has been better at taking risks, ignoring naysayers, overcoming fear or adapting to unfortunate circumstances.

We no longer need to personally know a 50-year-old who started a global non-profit, a 96-year-old who just graduated from college or a 70-year-old heart transplant recipient who climbed Mount Everest in order to understand that all these things are possible because others have done them. Inspiration now finds us wherever we live through social media channels and online communities.

I always take a video camera with me to masters swimming meets because it's a 100 percent certainty that there'll be dozens of inspiring stories to share. At a recent Rowdy Gaines Master's Classic swimming meet in Orlando, a relay team from Jacksonville was attempting to break a world record in the 360-plus age group. That means their combined age had to be at least 360. The team consisted of 93-year-old John Corse, 92-year-old Ed Graves, 89-year-old Betty Lorenzi and 86-year-old Joan Campbell.

All four had battled serious health setbacks, including cancer, heart disease and one broken neck among many other diseases, injuries and infirmities. "Way too many to mention," Ed said. But not only did they break the record, they smashed it, receiving a standing ovation from the crowd and bringing meet host Rowdy Gaines to tears. "It means a lot to me that they came to my meet and showed us all what active longevity looks like," he said.

We posted the video of their record-breaking race on the Growing Bolder Facebook page, and within 48 hours it had more than 7 million views, generated 54,000 comments and was shared 310,000 times. That's the power of social media, and the reason Growing Bolder believes in telling stories of ordinary people living extraordinary lives.

Niche online communities now exist for nearly every passion, problem, interest and ailment imaginable. You name it, there's a community built around it — and it's instantly accessible to anyone, anywhere in the world. So don't think that you're alone, because you're not. There are not only individuals like you; there are large virtual communities of people like you. Find them, join them and seek out those who are successfully doing what you'd like to do, or those who are overcoming a challenge that you're facing. Find "someone like me, only better."

11. Practice Visualization

Much has been written about the power of visualization. And I'm a big believer in it, especially when it comes to aging — an area in which it's almost never applied. Basically, visualization is imagining, in great detail, the feeling of successfully completing a task. It's a shortcut to success because the brain is incapable of telling the difference between real success and vividly imagined success.

Visualization convinces us that not only are we capable of performing in the imagined way, we've actually performed in the imagined way many times and have learned from the experience. The iconic "basketball study" has been used countless times to illustrate the power of visualization.

Dr. Judd Biasiotto conducted the study at the University of Chicago. "Dr. Judd," as he's referred to, split his subjects into three groups and tested each group on how many free throws they could make. For the next 30 days, people in the first group practiced free-throw shooting for an hour every day. People in the second group never took a shot — they only imagined shooting. They closed their eyes and visualized standing at the free-throw line, bouncing the ball, taking a deep breath, pulling the ball to their chests, focusing on the back of the rim and launching perfect shots that swished through the hoop. The third group was the control group; its members did nothing basketball related during the study period.

After 30 days, all three groups were tested again. The first group improved by 24 percent after practicing every day. The second group improved by 23 percent without ever having touched a basketball. And, as expected, the third group didn't improve at all. What the mind believes, the body embraces.

As you plan your comeback, take time to visualize the success you desire. Imagine the feeling of playing a piano, finishing a triathlon, losing weight, stopping smoking, recovering from surgery or making new friends. Imagine how you'll positively respond to setbacks, pain and negative feedback. Imagine an unshakeable determination to succeed, one in which you eliminate the option not to.

And don't stop there. Practice positive aging visualization. This is one of the most powerful and important tools for defeating the Machine and reprogramming your belief system. Visualize yourself growing stronger, not weaker, as you age. Visualize yourself becoming more active, more social, more flexible and more resilient. Visualize yourself saying yes to opportunity. If your mind believes it, so will your body.

While visualization is a powerful and useful technique, it's impossible to effectively visualize something that you don't believe is truly possible. If you aren't open to the *possibility* of changing your overall belief system about aging, visualization will be an ineffective waste of time.

12. Embrace Change and Impermanence

We need to embrace the impermanence of life because we are all ephemerals. We're lightning bugs and dandelions. Our time here is passing and precious. All things, good and bad, are transitory. Once we embrace our impermanence, we're able to let our achievements go as easily as we let go of our pain and suffering. Remember previous achievements or failures with fondness or regret, but don't allow them to become who you are, which automatically makes you into who you were. Allow them to help inform your future but never to tether you to the past.

We can't become the rock that clings to the bottom of the river and over time is worn smooth by the currents of life passing over us. We need to enter the current of life understanding that we can then steer ourselves in any direction. We won't always know exactly where we are going or what is around the next bend, but we won't be stuck to the bottom watching life race by. Bob Hope said, "I've always been in the right place and time. Of course, I steered myself there."

As adults over 60 transition into this new life stage, it's important to possess a willingness to not only embrace change, but to anticipate and adapt to it. Change is a constant, and the pace of change accelerates as we grow older. Unfortunately, most of us develop a debilitating case of change aversion. How many times have you heard someone describe an older person as "set in his ways" or "set in her ways?"

Since change is constant, it's also somewhat predictable. From a business or personal-interest perspective, change is the wave that we can ride to *what's next*. The question we must always be asking and answering is: "How is change affecting my areas of interest or expertise?"

Whether we realize it or not, we possess valuable inside information that makes forecasting change relatively easy. We discuss and strategize around change every day with our bosses, our teams, our families, our friends and our spouses. Once you acknowledge that change is coming and recognize where it's headed — get there.

Get there ahead of the change, or in the early stages of the change, because opportunity is change's constant companion. They move together, side-by-side. One begets the other. That's how real estate investors make fortunes. That's how clever ideas become small businesses and how small businesses become global empires. Change is your friend, because it can be predicted and leveraged.

Of course, not all change is good. That's why adaptability is a critical skill to develop. Adaptability enables us to change ourselves when we can't change our situation. We know physical changes are coming. We know that we'll eventually lose some mobility. We know that we'll eventually have to stop driving. Anticipating these life changes enables us to adjust our attitudes and expectations. That way, when changes come we're not blindsided or devastated. We're ready to adapt and move on.

If we can't embrace change and become adaptable, we won't be happy in old age.

13. Downsize *Now*

If you haven't already, begin downsizing. Start the transition from accumulating stuff to getting rid of stuff. As we age, when it comes to "things," less is more. No one ever says, "I wish I didn't begin downsizing so soon." It's nearly a universal sentiment that "I waited too long to downsize."

The *Los Angeles Times* reports that there are 300,000 items in the average American home. And that's just in the home. More than 25 percent of people whose homes have two-car garages don't have room to park even one car inside. And that's still not enough room. Self-storage has been the fastest growing segment of the U.S. commercial real estate industry over the past four decades, with $38 billion a year in revenues.

At some point we don't own stuff, it owns us. I'm not suggesting that we adopt the radical minimalist lifestyle of an acerbic monk — unless that's your thing. I am suggesting that we take a step or two in that direction. Declutter. Unburden yourself. Let go of the chase for material possessions.

Growing Bolder is about disconnecting from the mental manipulation inflicted upon us by advertisers. And it's no longer just advertisers telling us what our lives should look like — it's also the Facebook and Instagram feeds of our friends. Keeping up with the Joneses was never more difficult or less important. Let it go.

In our final days, none of us mourn the fact that we'll soon be separated from our stuff. As we grow older, our attachment to things weakens and our appreciation of experiences deepens.

14. Love Is the Answer

It makes no difference what the question is. Love is the answer. Love is the undefeated, undisputed heavyweight champion of the world. It's never been knocked out or even knocked down. Love is always the way forward and the path through. Through what? Anything. Everything. It makes no difference.

A wise physician once said: "The best medicine for humans

is love." But what if it doesn't work? "Increase the dose," the physician said. Researchers say he was right. Love raises our immunity, lowers our blood pressure and reduces our stress and depression. And it doesn't have to be the romantic kind of love. Close friendships and loving family have the same effect.

Love is not only good for our health; it's critical to our happiness. The two most common questions we ask ourselves just before death are "Was I loved?" and "Did I love?" In other words, love is the true source of happiness.

Don't make the mistake of saying, "I'll be happy when I have more money or when I achieve my goal." Because you won't be. The secret is realizing that we already have everything we need to be truly happy — the ability to love and to be loved.

15. Eat a Plant-Based Diet and Manage Your Microbiome

Many large, profit-obsessed companies aren't just stealing our futures by instilling the belief that we're weak, inadequate and of little value. They're also spending billions of dollars every year to persuade us to consume food that can lead to chronic illness, premature aging and an early death.

These companies are part of the Machine and actively engage in campaigns of misinformation to convince us that their products are a pathway to health and happiness when, in fact, they provide little value at best and are slowly killing us at worst. The modern American diet has led to an epidemic of arterial inflammation leading to heart disease and other silent killers.

Dr. Daniel Amen said this in his eye-opening book, "The Brain Warrior's Way": "The real weapons of mass destruction in our society are foods that are highly processed, pesticide sprayed, artificially colored and sweetened, high glycemic, low-fiber, food-like substances, laden with hormones, tainted with antibiotics."

It's important to understand that the food industry — like all industries — hires scientists, doctors, bloggers, journalists and marketing teams to report information favorable to their product or service. If we search long enough, we can find an "expert" with an impressive degree who'll confirm whatever belief or bias we hold — no matter how outrageous, dangerous or unhealthy it might be.

Do you want to believe that eating bacon is good for you (and who doesn't)? Then type "bacon is good for you" into Google. Dozens of official-looking articles describing the many health benefits of bacon appear, including one that claims: "Since it improves memory, bacon is a great addition to breakfast during the school years. Since it contains a high level of nutrients, it is a useful addition to any diet."

Your bias confirmed, you'll now feel good about eating as much bacon as you want and serving it to your kids — even though the World Health Organization, after reviewing more than 800 studies from 10 countries, has officially classified all processed meats as carcinogens.

Our diets have changed more in the past 100 years than they did in the previous 10,000 years. We're digging our graves with our teeth.

What do we really know about healthy eating and what kind of diet best supports active longevity? Growing Bolder has interviewed countless nutritionists, longevity experts, researchers and physicians. Among them, there's a universally strong and growing preference for plant-based diets. Plant-based diets have been proven to significantly decrease the chance of cardiovascular disease, cancer and diabetes. Dr. Richard

Carmona, the 17th surgeon general of the United States, said: "The best advice is what your grandmother told you years ago. Eat your greens. Grandma was correct, and we have the science to prove it."

A plant-based diet encourages gut heath, which may be the most important health trend in medical science in the past two decades. Gut health generally refers to the state of the microbiome — an ecosystem of more than 1,000 different species of bacteria living in your gut.

There are more bacterial cells in your body (an estimated 40 trillion) than human cells (about 30 trillion.) Our microbiomes are as individual as our fingerprints and have a direct impact on aging, mood, digestion, the immune system and cognitive function.

What makes the microbiome so important to overall health is the gut's complex relationship to the brain through the enteric nervous system (ENS). The ENS, commonly referred to as the "second brain," is a network of nerves, neurons and neurotransmitters — much like the brain itself — that lines the gut and is hardwired to the brain. The ENS regulates brain chemistry, stress responses, anxiety and memory through its response to the endless array of chemical reactions taking place within the microbiome.

Our microbiomes are constantly changing due to many factors, including diet. The more diverse the bacteria in our gut, the more health benefits we receive. Plant-based diets that include a wide variety of fruits, vegetables, whole grains and fermented foods produce the most diverse microbiomes.

Protein is important as we age. But most animal proteins have been found to increase the risk of mortality. High-protein foods derived from plants, such as beans and nuts, provide the same benefit without the same effect on mortality.

The simple dietary prescription for active longevity is all things in moderation. When and where we can, we should reduce calories, limit animal proteins and eliminate highly processed foods.

16. Get Active and Demand Extreme Recovery

If we want to keep moving, then we must simply keep moving. This statement irritates people who don't want to exercise and believe those who do are denying the realities of growing older. After all, they say, exercise doesn't *guarantee* a longer life.

Longevity may or may not be a side benefit of physical activity. But that's not why we exercise. We exercise because it makes us feel good today. We exercise because it improves the quality of our life tomorrow. We exercise because it makes us happier. We exercise because it reduces our healthcare costs. If exercise also helps us live longer or, through compressed morbidity, die faster, that's simply an added benefit.

That said, being active isn't just about movement. Being active is about engagement. It's about building friendships, being involved in our communities, pursuing our passions and remaining relevant.

If every setback strips us of some ability, some degree of mobility or some level of social engagement, then the cumulative effects ultimately rob us of the potential for active longevity. It's imperative to recover from every setback as fully as possible. At times, that requires what can only be described as extreme recovery.

Extreme recovery requires extreme dedication. But its benefits go far beyond simply returning us to an active life. Extreme recovery is a Growing Bolder booster shot that disrupts the

Machine and inoculates us against its lies.

An important facilitator of extreme recovery is prehabilitation — preparing for the inevitable setbacks that we all will face as we grow older (see Chapter 12).

17. Travel

The more we value experience, the more interested we become in travel. In a survey of baby boomers that asked about regrets (chances not taken and dreams not realized), most respondents (56 percent) said they would "travel extensively" if they had 30 extra years. News flash: Most of us do have an extra 30 years.

Travel is the perfect jump-starter for "what's next." It gives us perspective, provides us inspiration and increases our empathy and compassion. It charges our physical, emotional, spiritual and creative batteries and helps us think outside the box.

Bucket lists for those age 50 and older might include visiting an ancestor's homeland, running a marathon, learning a new language, climbing a mountain, hiking the Inca trail, taking a European river cruise, joining a mission trip or seeing a polar bear in the wild. The sky's the limit.

Wherever we travel becomes a part of us, which is why experiential travel is the booming travel trend. Older travelers now dominate the travel industry — and increasingly, they're not simply sightseers. They absorb the culture — immersing themselves in the history, food, geography and people of whatever destination they've chosen.

Adventure travel is booming in part thanks to technology, which diminishes the perception of risk that has, in the past, kept many older people at home. A satellite phone, or even a cell phone, and a decent travel insurance policy make the idea of hiking a remote wilderness trail in a foreign country far less frightening. Older travelers are now more willing to accept the risk of a broken bone or other health emergency with the knowledge that they can be airlifted out in a matter of hours if something goes wrong.

Embrace the transformative power of travel and don't think you're too old to enjoy its many benefits. The sharpest growth in the travel industry has been in the over-85 crowd — up more than 70 percent in the last 10 years. The world's a big place. What are you waiting for?

18. Be Curious and Embrace the Gig Economy

One of the keys to successful aging is transforming fear into curiosity. Curiosity might have killed the cat but it's critically important to maintaining our health and wellbeing. A lack of curiosity means acceptance of the status quo, which in an ageist culture is highly destructive. A lack of curiosity leads to complacency and resistance to change, while embracing curiosity leads to lifelong learning. Curiosity is one of mankind's most important characteristics and is responsible for every great invention and advancement in history. Albert Einstein said, "I have no special talents, I'm just passionately curious."

A great place to indulge your curiosity is the internet. Not only is it the greatest lifelong learning tool in history, I believe it represents the greatest post-retirement revenue-creation opportunity that has ever existed. It will enable people in their 70s, 80s and 90s to supplement their incomes, monetize their passions and create new businesses through the gig economy.

The gig economy enables a rapidly growing trend toward contract workers and individual "gigs." It can include opportunities in writing, marketing, customer service, research and more. The gig economy has previously been called the "sharing economy" in reference to home-sharing and ride-sharing companies like Airbnb and Uber. The gig economy is primarily driven by app-based platforms that allow anyone to benefit from the services offered via these platforms or to provide their own offerings to a massive online marketplace. It provides easy and open access to markets and industries that have historically been controlled by large corporate interests. A quarter of all workers in the gig economy are 50 and older, a percentage that is likely to steadily grow in the years ahead.

Taking advantage of the ever-increasing opportunities of the gig economy requires an ability to access and manage the applications and platforms that these opportunities are built upon. That won't be a challenge for those now in their 20s and 30s, who grew up with the internet and mobile devices. For those who didn't, the challenge is to catch up — but that's on us.

Take a class, hire a mentor, make it happen. That's Growing Bolder.

19. Let Your Freak Flag Fly

In their 1970 album "Déjà Vu," Crosby, Stills, Nash & Young sing about letting your freak flag fly — a metaphor for being who you are and not trying to conform to the expectations of others. The song became an anthem for hippies worldwide. We must all let our freak flags fly as we grow older, because conforming to the current norm of aging will more than likely prevent us from becoming our true selves.

Everyone is unique, of course. But most of us, over the years, have had our weirdness, creativity and unconventional individuality squeezed out. As we grow older, we need to nurture that which makes us unique. In other words, give ourselves permission to be our true selves. Fitting in isn't the goal. Pleasing others isn't the motivation. We must create our own definitions of success and then go get them.

If life is a masquerade, this is the time to remove our masks and let our true colors shine. Doing so will open doors that we never knew existed. This is the time to let our freak flags fly. If not now, when?

20. Leave a Legacy

One of our Growing Bolder mantras is "Move Forward. Give Back." We believe a passion for helping others and making a difference is one of the most important keys to successful aging.

Many are overwhelmed at the thought of legacy. Who am I to leave a legacy? What can I possibly leave behind that can make a difference? These thoughts are another byproduct of systematic brainwashing, through which we've gradually been led to believe that our value depreciates as we age, and that ultimately, we have very little to offer to anyone else.

Leaving a legacy doesn't require much time, any money or even valuable skills. The legacy doesn't have to be something that will dramatically change the planet or better mankind. Arthur Ashe said: "Start where you are. Use what you have. Do what you can."

We never know when an encouraging word may change the course of someone's life or add value to the world. That encouraging word can be your legacy — but only if you give it. Mahatma Gandhi said, "The best way to find yourself is to lose yourself in the service of others." John Wooden, the great Hall of Fame basketball coach, said, "You can't live a perfect day without doing something for someone who will never be able to repay you." We're responsible not only for serving others, but for protecting the planet and its finite natural resources for future generations. To ensure the future of mankind, every generation — and every individual — is responsible for creating more than it consumes. This is one of our greatest opportunities to leave a legacy.

Leaving a meaningful legacy can be as simple as encouraging others, protecting the planet or simply living a life that inspires others. Enthusiasm for our passions is enthusiasm for life — and that's infectious, contagious and a powerful legacy.

Inspirational author Shannon L. Adler put it this way: "Carve your name on hearts, not tombstones. A legacy is etched into the minds of others and the stories they share about you."

In the end, our legacies are simply the stories people tell about us when we're gone. What stories will they tell about you?

21. Pursue your Spirituality

For centuries, many of the world's greatest scientists, philosophers and religious leaders have pondered the mystery and the meaning of death. If there's one answer, one explanation, one solution and one reality, then why are there so many different beliefs and interpretations?

How can one religion be right and all the others wrong? How can one group of God-loving believers be granted access to heaven and eternal bliss while another group of God-loving believers are excluded? How can the country in which we were born, or the people who raised us, taught us or governed us, determine whether we're worthy of eternal life?

We live in a world in which religion has become something that divides us. But spirituality is something that can unite us. Religion grew out of spirituality. Therefore, at their core, all religions are basically the same — or were the same when they were founded. Only their stories and their adherents are different. Over the centuries, our interpretations, cultures and languages gradually created differences in religious doctrine. And these differences have spawned division, hate and wars.

This isn't to say that we should leave our churches, mosques and temples, abandon our religions or ignore our priests, pastors, rabbis, mullahs, gurus or whomever we consider spiritual leaders. We should celebrate our religions, because they were born of truth and noble intention. But we must understand that all religions have been corrupted, to some degree, by their practitioners. We can't allow the frustration, friction and turmoil created by religion to prevent us from connecting with our spirituality — because spirituality recognizes the truth in all religions.

Spirituality is our relationship with the divine without the middleman. It's a deeply personal experience with life, existence and consciousness. It's a personal path to enlightenment. While we pursue our spirituality, we should also encourage and support others in their pursuits. Because we're all flawed sinners on a journey of discovery. Ram Dass, the American spiritual teacher, says it best: "When all is said and done, we're all just walking each other home."

It's Your Move

I'm constantly amazed at the battle between the anti-aging/reverse-aging proponents and the "aging sucks, just accept it" proponents. Both ideas are far from reality and equally damaging. It's either a pie-in-the-sky pursuit of unachievable immortality or a demoralizing acceptance of the unalterable fact of physiological decline.

There are an increasing number of books in which the authors painstakingly describe in great biological detail "the spectacle of decomposition." These books, a reaction to the countless uber-positive "you can live forever" books, seem to revel in the unavoidable degradation of human physiology. The authors sound like outraged prosecutors presenting their final arguments as they attempt to convince juries that aging is little more than a disgusting physical demise, characterized by leaky cells, brittle bones, clogged arteries, painful joints and out-of-control inflammation: "Ladies and gentlemen of the jury, attempting to slow or mitigate the impact of aging makes the defendant guilty of foolish naivety."

This is an easy one, my friends. There's a huge and malleable middle ground that offers both truth and optimism. There's an achievable reality not built upon fantastical falsehoods or disheartening resignation. You can, in fact, be happy and fulfilled until you draw your final breath.

I often say that age isn't a disease, it's an opportunity. It would be more accurate to say that age isn't a disease *unless we believe it to be*, in which case it will most assuredly become a disease. Likewise, age isn't an opportunity *unless we believe it to be*. Whether we want it or not, whether we decide to wield it or not, we have the power to decide if growing older is a disease or an opportunity. If you decide that it is, indeed, an opportunity, then you and only you get to define what that opportunity is.

The key to growing older is to not mourn what's lost but to celebrate what remains, not to identify with loss and limitation but to embrace passion and possibility. Growing Bolder is about accepting the realities of our mortality but rejecting the lies of our ageist culture.

Growing Bolder begins with changing our belief systems about growing older. This would be difficult enough if we lived in a vacuum, but in reality we are part of an overtly and aggressively ageist culture that seems to be growing more mean-spirited by the day. Generational finger pointing has never been more rampant, and while we battle for inclusion, the ethic in ascendance today is exclusion. It's open season on old people, sick people, poor people, people of color, people from other countries and people of different religions.

A society that turns away from the poor and the sick isn't going to suddenly experience a large-scale revelation about the value of older people and the opportunities of growing older. That change will occur slowly, one person at a time.

The good news is, we can all be that person. Because the truth — and the magic — is this: If we can change our belief systems about growing older, we can change how we age. We can transform our future from decades of loss and limitation to decades of passion, purpose and possibility.

Let me ask you an important question. When you imagine yourself living longer, do you see yourself as being older longer or younger longer? If your answer is "older longer," you are under the control of the Machine and being directed by ageist autopilot that will define and control your final decades. We must switch off the autopilot, take the controls and navigate toward the future we want. We might not actually arrive at our imagined destination but the journey toward it will be filled with interest, meaning, challenge, excitement, frustration, love and friendship — the stuff of life.

GROWING BOLDER IS ABOUT belief, desire, dedication and persistence. We must believe that there can be more, desire to have more, dedicate ourselves to achieving more and persist in our efforts to create more. If that sounds like work, it is. It's the best work you can get. It's the most rewarding, satisfying and life-enriching work possible.

We must go forward with excitement and enthusiasm, knowing that our potential is unlimited — no matter the decade or life stage in which we find ourselves. We must never allow the outside world, the media, our insecurities, our friends or even the time and effort already invested in achieving one thing prevent us from changing course and trying something else. We must stretch ourselves, meet new people and consider alternative views on everything. Flexibility of body and mind is an important ingredient in active longevity.

Remember, medicine is not healthcare. Medicine is sick care. Good food, vigorous exercise, great friends, sound sleep and mental stimulation are healthcare.

Remember above all else: what the mind believes, the body embraces. Our psychological health drives our physiological health. We anticipate the perceived negative benchmarks of growing older so powerfully that we guarantee they'll come to pass — and the result is devastating on a personal and societal level. We're literally killing ourselves with our belief systems, robbing ourselves of not only years of life but quality of life, and adding billions of dollars to our national healthcare costs.

Life is about learning, and the last great task is learning how to grow older. Growing Bolder isn't about changing what is true — it's about finding the power and the possibility in what is happening.

How do I define successful aging? Never stop growing. More specifically, never stop Growing Bolder. Close your eyes and imagine someone who is 60, 80 or even 100. Now imagine more. A lot more. Now go make it happen.

I close with my wishes for you.

May You ...

- *Always believe that the rest of your life can be the best of your life.*

- *Live fearlessly with passion and purpose, leaning into life's biggest challenges with optimism and determination.*

- *Have faith in the power of your dreams and in your ability to realize them.*

- *Feel like an important part of the human family, experiencing the joy of true human connection with people of all ages, races and religions.*

- *Embrace the ephemeral nature of life while feeling a timeless, boundless and infinite connection to all of creation.*

- *Strive to live in the moment, learning from — but not being controlled by — your past and always remaining excited about your future.*

- *Allow yourself to experience endless moments of joy, understanding that happiness can only be found in the journey and not in the destination.*

- *Feel and express a deep gratitude for all that you have and be inspired by a desire to make a difference in the lives of others.*

- *Feel a true connection to our fragile planet and a deep obligation to protect its beauty and ensure its health for future generations.*

- *Make lifestyle choices that can improve the quality of your life until the very end, and when the end comes ...*

- *Surrender with dignity and find yourself surrounded by love, filled with peace and curious to discover what's next.*

- *Experience the deep satisfaction of knowing that you showed those you love not only how to live but also how to die.*

ACKNOWLEDGMENTS

———

This book was written in four-hour blocks, every Saturday and Sunday morning for two years, while sitting in a booth at Panera Bread eating a double-toasted everything bagel and drinking hazelnut coffee. I thank Panera for a comfortable workspace and what adds up to 208 bagels and 208 cups of fresh coffee over that two-year period.

Randy Noles is a Florida publishing icon who helped launch our magazine and was kind enough to clean up my original manuscript before passing it on to his colleague, Michael Mc-Cleod, who also provided valuable input.

We publish a magazine and I was determined that this would be the first book from Growing Bolder Publishing. Of course, we needed help and guidance at every turn, and for that I'm thankful to Bob Morris and his team at Story Farm. Bob is a former newspaper columnist, magazine editor and successful novelist who, in a very Growing Bolder move, took a major leap of faith to start a publishing company that creates "enduring, story-driven legacies for a select group of accomplished clients." I'm proud to be one of those clients.

I'm beyond grateful to the leadership team at Growing Bolder including Bill Shafer, Jackie Carlin, Katy Widrick, Jason Morrow, Mike Nanus, and Jill Middleton. This book is as much theirs as mine.

I'm a big believer that the right people show up at the right time if you're aware enough to recognize and appreciate their value. I'm grateful to Robert Thompson for being one of those people and bringing with him the amazingly talented designer Ashley Heafy and the brilliant Emily Thompson. Together, they helped inform the look, feel and marketing of this book.

Growing Bolder would not be possible without my business partner Joe R. Lee. Joe's steadfast belief in our business mission has given me the determination to push through the countless obstacles that face any small business, especially one birthed during the historic economic collapse of 2008. Joe is a true global business icon who taught us that doing good is as important as doing well.

Finally, my deepest thanks to my family: Jill, Kelsey, and Quinn Middleton. Kelsey and Quinn really didn't do anything other than being themselves, but when you're kind, gentle, funny, brilliant souls who call me "Dad" that's more than enough. Jill has always embraced the journey's passion, enthusiasm and optimism. While I sat in Panera eating bagels and writing, she mowed the lawn and cleaned the pool and never once complained. And when I moaned and groaned about the enormity of the task, the lack of time to dedicate to it, and the possibility that I didn't have what it takes to finish it, Jill always smiled and said: "You'll get it done and it will be worth the effort." I needed to hear that every time she said it.

INDEX

McGuinn, Roger, 143
media
    age as a first-level identifier,
        51–52
    cultural hypnosis of
        commercials, 28–29
    negative portrayals of aging,
        27–28
    pervasiveness of ageist
        messages, 30–31
Medicaid, 135
Medicare, 134–135
medication and supplements
    DES (Diethylstilbestrol)
        exposure, 128–129
    direct-to-consumer (DTC)
        advertising, 83–84
    memory and brain health,
        178–179
    pharmaceutical industry
        spending, 83–84
    side effects, 84
    usage by centenarians, 75
Melov, Simon, 85–86
memory issues
    Alzheimer's disease, 178–180,
        183–187
    author's family's experiences
        with Alzheimer's
        disease, 183–187
    benefits of creativity and art
        therapy, 114–115
    Brain Fitness Club, 180–182
    dementia, 178
    destigmatizing, 179–182
Meyer, Molly Middleton, 184–187
microbiomes, 236
Middleton, Marc
    broadcast news career, 8–9,
        11–14
    efforts to change views on
        aging, 11–12
    and the Growing Bolder

    movement, 2, 24–25,
        228–229
    Mount Kilimanjaro trip,
        156–160
    personal wishes for the reader,
        247
    swimming workout, 219–220,
        225–226
    thoughts about death, 201
Middleton, Tom, 183–184
MIT AgeLabs three questions
        exercise regarding aging
        in place, 194–196
mitochondria, 88, 110
Morris, Hugh, 128
Mount Kilimanjaro trip, 156–160
mourning, 69–70
Muniz, Roselio, 72, 76, 127–128
muscle mass, 85–86
muscle memory, 125–126,
        224–227
myth of physical decline and loss
        of flexibility, 84–85
"My Time: Making the Most of
        the Bonus Decades after
        50" (article), 11

N

Naranjo, Gladys, 170–171
negativity, avoiding, 222–224
neurological benefits of exercise
    brain-derived neurotropic
        factor (BDNF), 110
    hippocampus, 89
    neurogenesis, 109–111
    Olga Kotelko example, 111–
        114
New England Centenarian Study,
        72
Nyad, Diana, 52

O

obesity, 73–74